About the Authors

Pat Pridmore is a member of the Education and International Development (EID) academic group at the Institute of Education, University of London. She has been a member of the research and training groups of the Child-to-Child Trust in London. She has over twenty years' experience of working in international education, health and nutrition, mostly in East, West and Southern African countries. In 1989 she joined the staff of the Institute of Education in London, where she is currently a lecturer in health promotion and development. She is regularly engaged as a consultant in the areas of school health, programme evaluation and medical education and has worked in this capacity in Swaziland, Botswana, Kenya, India, Vietnam and Saudi Arabia. She is the co-author of *Stepping Forward: Children and Young People Participating* (Intermediate Technology, 1998) and is currently preparing a book on participatory planning (Macmillan, forthcoming).

David Stephens is Professor of International Education at Oslo College in Norway, and was until recently a member of the Centre for International Education at the Institute of Education at the University of Sussex. He has also served as chairperson of the Child-to-Child Partnership Committee based in London. For the past twenty-five years he has lectured and researched in international education in universities in East and West Africa and in the UK. His most recent co-authored publications include *Doing Educational Research in Developing Countries* (Falmer, 1990) and *Questions of Quality, Primary Education and Development* (Longman, 1990). He is presently completing a book on culture in education and development.

About the Book

This book takes a careful, objective view of the many activities that have been set up by Child-to-Child. It contains a very useful literature review of evaluation studies of Child-to-Child activities and programmes. The examples of high-quality work in which children play a key role in the promotion of health are truly inspirational. The work of Child-to-Child is now seen to be a key component of any community-based project.

The book is very clearly written with many excellent examples, which can be applied in different situations. It is essential reading for anybody involved in Primary Health Care or Education.

Andrew Tomkins, Professor of International Child Health, Institute of Child Health, University of London

The Child-to-Child programme has been one of the most important international school health promotion initiatives in recent years. This excellent book will be a valuable resource for anyone wanting a critical assessment of its achievements, strengths and weaknesses.

John Hubley, author of Communicating Health: an action guide to health education and health promotion, Macmillan/TALC, 1993

This book is a comprehensive and insightful review of the literature and evolution, including the adaptations and impact, of the Child-to-Child participatory programme approach over the last 20 years. It serves as an invaluable resource guide to anyone working in primary health care or involved in health promotion or educational activities at the community level. It is very well written and rich with concrete examples about what has worked and what has not worked in different cultural and environmental settings throughout the world. A 'must' read for anyone working or interested in human resource development.

Carol Hoppy, Human Development Officer, World Bank, Washington DC

Children as Partners for Health
A critical review of the child-to-child approach

Pat Pridmore and David Stephens

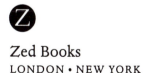

Zed Books
LONDON • NEW YORK

Children as Partners for Health: A critical review of the child-to-child approach was first published by Zed Books Ltd, 7 Cynthia Street, London N1 9JF, UK and Room 400, 175 Fifth Avenue, New York, NY 10010, USA in 2000.

Distributed exclusively in the USA by St Martin's Press, Inc., 175 Fifth Avenue, New York, NY 10010, USA.

Cover designed by Lee Robinson/Ad Lib Design, London N19
Set in Monotype Dante by Ewan Smith, London
Printed and bound in Malaysia

A catalogue record for this book is available from the British Library

Library of Congress Cataloging-in-Publication Data
Pridmore, Pat, 1947–
    Children as partners for health: a critical review of the child-to-child approach/Pat Pridmore and David Stephens.
      p. cm
    Includes bibliographical references and index.
    ISBN 1-85649-635-X (cased) — ISBN 1-85649-636-8 (limp)
    1. School children—Health and hygiene—Case studies.
    2. Health education—Case studies. I. Stephens, David, 1950– .
    II. Title.
    LB1587.A3 P75 1999
    371'1—dc21
                              99-052797

ISBN 1 85649 635 x cased
ISBN 1 85649 636 8 limp

Contents

Figures and Tables

Figures

Table

Acknowledgements

From the outset of this book we have been privileged to work with dedicated, enthusiastic and supportive friends and colleagues from three continents. We wish to thank Sonal Zaveri, director of the Centre for Research and Development, Bombay, India; Sue Occleston, director of Shared Learning in Action, UK; and Mags Petkiewicz, co-ordinator of Niño a Niño, Oaxaca, Mexico, for providing material for case studies. We also wish to thank our editor, Robert Molteno, for his continual support and encouragement, and Hugh Hawes for sharing his ideas and experiences of Child-to-Child and writing the Foreword. We are deeply indebted to our families for allowing us to have the personal space needed to complete the manuscript.

As co-authors we have read and criticized each other's work and edited successive drafts. Chapters 1, 2, 3, 4 and 8 are written by Pat Pridmore and based on her PhD thesis. Chapter 5 is written by David Stephens. Material for the case studies in Chapters 6 and 7 was provided by Sonal Zaveri (India), Sue Occleston (UK), Pat Pridmore (Botswana) and David Stephens (Uganda and Ghana).

To all those who took part in and have helped this work in any way – we thank you.

Foreword

A new book describing and updating the Child-to-Child movement is overdue, and I am pleased to see that it has now emerged.

Those interested in describing and publicizing Child-to-Child have always had a problem in choosing their audiences. Should the book appeal to general readers, as did CHILD-to-child (Aarons et al. 1979) or to the academic community? This book is clearly targeted to the latter. It is written by two university teachers from London and Sussex who both have a considerable experience over the last ten years of working with and alongside schools and communities using the Child-to-Child approach. It is well documented and comprehensive, and contains a number of useful case studies deriving from the specific experience of the authors. Since the approach is used in such a variety of countries and in such a number of ways, these are bound to be selective, a fact that the authors themselves recognize.

The book has another great advantage over certain other descriptions of the movement. It is written with a considerable degree of objectivity: it points out the ambiguities and weaknesses of the Child-to-Child message and approach as well as their value and appeal, and indicates the considerable difficulties already experienced by those who seek to see the dream of children as a major force in health promotion turn into a widespread reality.

One of the concerns of this book is that the movement remains too dependent on the influence of its initiators even though, as it admits, these have done everything in their power to pass the initiative to others. As one of these initiators, I would like to comment briefly on this view.

When Child-to-Child was launched in 1979, its scope and aspirations were far more modest than those later claimed for the movement and presented in this book. The concept of Primary Health Care newly set out in the Alma Ata conference (see WHO 1978) led to the realization that when 'people' are encouraged to take greater responsibility for their own health and to spread new ideas and practices to others, 'people' need to be seen to include children. At one of the early workshops, talk was of a 'bag of ideas', describing ways in which children could make a difference to the health of others. It was envisaged that this 'bag' would be raided for different reasons and to different degrees by different people in different circumstances. It was on this principle that the Activity Sheets – still, to my mind, the greatest resource produced by Child-to-Child – were produced.

Later, partly due to the rapid spread of the activities and the interest in them, particularly at universities and international agencies, Child-to-Child acquired a recommended approach, a methodology, principles – even, in some people's eyes, a philosophy. We implemented Child-to-Child and had 'Child-to-Child programmes and projects', which needed to be evaluated, hence repeated requests to 'evaluate Child-to-Child', a virtual impossibility. The methodology was characterized as either more or less community- and activity-based. We counted gains and mourned losses to the Child-to-Child family round the world. It is this view of Child-to-Child that this book examines.

Over the past 20 years, I have seen this canon accumulating, with interest, wonder and occasionally alarm when I have seen dogmatism creeping in. Undoubtedly much of it is here to stay, but when we read this new book about Child-to-Child and form our own opinions as to its successes and failures, let us also keep in mind the two original goals: the 'bag of ideas' and the 'let's include the children too' principle. There is no need for a programme or an activity to be overtly 'Child-to-Child' to use its ideas or elements of the methodology. It is for this reason that I am very pleased to note that the book recognizes the value of a Child-to-Child element within a policy of developing health-promoting schools and gives credit to the Trust's decision, made some years ago, to make such a policy one of the central priorities in its publication and training programme.

Hugh Hawes, Reader Emeritus, Institute of Education,
University of London and former director, Child-to-Child Trust

Abbreviations and Acronyms

AIDS	acquired immuno-deficiency syndrome
AKF	Aga Khan Foundation
AMREF	African Medical Research and Education Foundation
ANPCCAN	African Network for the Protection and Prevention Against Child Abuse
ARC	Arab Resource Collective
BERA	Botswana Educational Research Association
CHETNA	Centre for Health Education Training and Nutrition Awareness
CISAS	Centre for Information and Advisory Services in Health (a Nicaraguan NGO)
DfID	Department for International Development (UK) (formerly known as the Overseas Development Administration, ODA)
GNP	gross national product
HDI	Human Development Index
HIV	human immuno-deficiency virus
HRD	human resource development
ICCB	International Catholic Children's Bureau
IEDE	Institute of Education, Development and Extension
ITEK	Institute of Teacher Education at Kyambogo
MCH	maternal and child health
NFE	non-formal education
NGO	non-governmental organization
ODA	Overseas Development Administration (UK) (now Department for International Development, DfID)
PHC	Primary Health Care
PLA	Participatory Learning and Action

PRA	Participatory Rural Appraisal/Participatory Research Techniques
PTA	parent–teacher association
ORS	oral rehydration solution
RADs	remote area dwellers
SCF	Save the Children Fund
SHAP	School Health Action Plan
SHEP	School Health Education Project
TALC	Teaching Aids at Low Cost
UCEW	University College of Education at Winneba
UK	United Kingdom
UN	United Nations
UN ACC/SCN	United Nations Sub-Committee on Nutrition
UNDP	United Nations Development Programme
UNESCO	United Nations Educational, Scientific and Cultural Organization
UNICEF	United Nations Children's Fund
WCEFA	World Conference on Education for All
WHO	World Health Organization

This book is dedicated to all those who work with children and strive for health. When we work with children we not only change the present – we change the future.

We are all teachers

1. Schoolteachers
2. Parents
3. Older children with younger children
4. Religious leaders
5. Health workers
6. Craftsmen

Source: Aarons et al. 1979.

1

The Need for a Critical View of Child-to-Child

There are many books that describe the approach to health education known as Child-to-Child. In this book we take a rather different approach, in that we critically place Child-to-Child within a broader developmental context where a number of issues need to be addressed.

We analyse the extraordinary growth and development of Child-to-Child and examine case studies from different countries in order to show how successful implementation depends on detailed adaptation to the local context, and also to identify what still needs to be done to strengthen the approach. We aim to provide a cutting edge for those of us concerned with improving the situation of children by addressing issues of children's participation, new foci of development, new partnerships for health, the spread of 'Western' ideas around the world and the interface between education and health.

As we near the end of the millennium there is still much to be done to improve the state of the world's children. The following scenario illustrates the reality of life for many children today.

Her name is Amina, and she lives in sub-Saharan Africa in the dusty Sahel region, a world and a half away from the capital city. The good news is that she and her mother are survivors (971 maternal deaths per 1,000,000 live births) and that though she is under-nourished as a six-year-old (28,000,000 children estimated as malnourished in sub-Saharan Africa in 1997), she is loved and valued by her large extended family.

1

> *The bad news is that she is far less likely than her male relative to attend or remain in school, particularly if he lives in the more prosperous south of the country. She will spend a life burdened with home chores, preventable illness, and the shadow of poverty (Odaga and Heneveld 1995; Stephens 1998).*

Life for Amina hangs in the balance. This book is about Amina and her brothers and sisters and their future.

Child-to-Child Ideas and Methods

From the literature we can see that Child-to-Child is promoted as an innovative approach to basic learning and basic health care that both respects and challenges traditional attitudes. It builds on a tradition of children helping each other and their families and sharing their ideas, but rejects the low position traditionally occupied by children in the social hierarchy. It supports the tradition of children as partners in child care and child development, but also promotes them as partners in decision-making processes.

The underlying philosophy of Child-to-Child derives from a deep commitment to Primary Health Care (PHC), to the role of children as agents, and to the promotion of partnerships for health. The principle of PHC focuses on developing the power of individuals and communities to share responsibility for the improvement of their

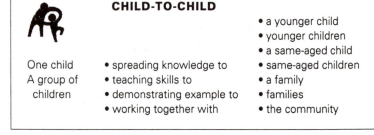

Figure 1.1 Children as agents of change (*source:* adapted from Child-to-Child 1994b: 6).

LEARNING AND DOING: LEARNING PLACE AND LIVING PLACE

Class/school   Home/community

Step 1

Recognize
Learning about diarrhoea and
dehydration.

Step 2

Study

(1) A survey at home and with
neighbours. Who suffers from it?
How is it treated?

(2) Discuss findings. Which
babies are most at risk? Which
local remedies are helpful?

Step 3

Act
(1) Plan action (How can
children help to prevent and
treat diarrhoea?)

(2) Helping mother at home
when the baby has
diarrhoea.Washing hands after
cleaning the baby's bottom.
Telling 'what we learnt at
school' why this is important.

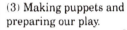

(3) Making puppets and
preparing our play.

(4) Performing the play in the
village square.

Step 4

Evaluate
(1) 'What did we do? How well
did our show work? Should we
change it next time?'

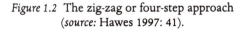

(2) 'Can we remember all we
learnt? Can we all make a
rehydration drink?'

(3) Carrying on with actions to
prevent and treat diarrhoea at
home.

Figure 1.2 The zig-zag or four-step approach
(*source*: Hawes 1997: 41).

Figure 1.3 The 'Facts for Life Bus' (*source*: Hawes and
Scotchmer 1993: 21).

own health. Child-to-Child aims to develop children as partners in
PHC. The principle of children as agents of change reflects faith in
the power of children to spread health messages and health practices
to younger children, peers, families and communities, together with
the conviction that they should enjoy and profit from doing so.
(Figure 1.1 provides a model of children as agents of change.)

Alongside the ideas that inform Child-to-Child, a step-by-step
educational process has been developed, informed by theories of
active learning and empowerment education. This process involves
awareness-raising, critical thinking, action and reflection, requiring in
turn:

- identifying a health issue;
- understanding the issue and its importance to children and their
  families;
- deciding and planning what action children can take and who can
  help them;
- taking action individually and together;
- discussing and evaluating results; and
- deciding how to do it better next time.

This process is depicted in Figure 1.2 as a four-step 'zig-zag' methodo-

Figure 1.4 Active methods for learning and teaching
(*source*: Hawes 1997: 43).

logy and in Figure 1.3 as the wheels of the 'Facts for Life' bus, with skills and competencies (shown as luggage) developed as the bus travels along.

As children are guided through this educational process by their teacher, different methods can be used to encourage children to understand health issues, communicate messages and evaluate the effects of their actions. Some of these methods are illustrated in Figure 1.4.

Child-to-Child: the Worldwide Movement

Child-to-Child ideas have spread with extraordinary rapidity around the world and have had considerable influence at all levels. Since the approach was first developed in 1978 a worldwide movement has built up involving more than eighty countries and a wide range of people from the powerful presidents of countries to grassroots health workers and teachers. The hope is that members of this vast network share a concern for the health and well-being of children and the desire for health and education to work together, and also possess the willingness to listen to ideas irrespective of status. A model of the movement is shown in Figure 1.5. The development of this network has been aided by the flexibility of the concept and the freedom allowed for local adaptation and for people to contribute new ideas and activities from their own experience.

At the tip of the pyramid is the Trust in London, supported by resource persons, and at the base are the millions of children (and the adults working with them) who are actively involved in using the ideas. At other levels of the movement are the international consultants who provide expertise at national and international levels, and those working in ministries of health and education to initiate and co-ordinate school health programmes. The intention is that the movement should be based on partnership and dialogue at all levels – an intention shared not least by the founders of the movement, even though, as we shall see, their personal standing remains such that they may often be deferred to. Within the movement the Trust helps to strengthen links within regions and countries. It acts as a clearing-house for information and has published directories of Child-

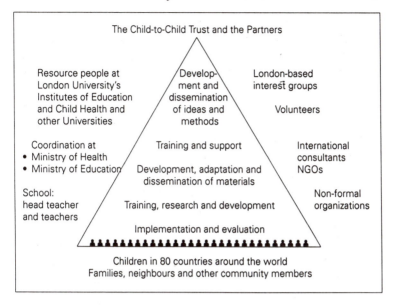

The Child-to-Child Trust and the Partners

Resource people at
London University's
Institutes of Education
and Child Health and
other Universities

Develop-
ment and
dissemination
of ideas and
methods

London-based
interest groups

Volunteers

Coordination at
• Ministry of Health
• Ministry of Education

Training and support

Development, adaptation and
dissemination of materials

International
consultants
NGOs

School:
head teacher
and teachers

Training, research and development

Implementation and evaluation

Non-formal
organizations

Children in 80 countries around the world
Families, neighbours and other community members

Figure 1.5 Child-to-Child: the worldwide movement

to-Child initiatives to disseminate details of activities and contact persons around the world (Child-to-Child 1993b, 1993c).

Although a more appropriate model for Child-to-Child might be circular (with all members of the movement holding hands in equal partnership), a triangular model is closer to current reality, acknowledging differences in power and resources between stakeholders.

Child-to-Child and Health Promotion in Our Schools

An upsurge of interest in school health has been encouraged by increasing evidence that it can be an effective strategy for improving both health and educational achievement (Pollitt 1990; UN ACC/ SCN 1990; Caldwell 1993). Interest in promoting health through primary schooling has been further boosted by the focus on Basic Education to achieve the goal of 'Education for All' adopted by the World Conference on Education in Jomtien, Thailand, in 1990.

Consequently, education planners and health planners are currently seeking to increase their understanding of the complex processes involved in successful implementation of health education programmes in different contexts. Supporters of Child-to-Child believe that they have found an approach that can harness the power of children to promote health and that is sufficiently flexible to be adapted to the local context and be owned by participants. Child-to-Child views classroom activities against the background of the school as a health-promoting environment, and seeks to strengthen the bridge between the school and the community.

Despite increased interest, school health education is still struggling for legitimacy as an effective and efficient strategy for improving health. Planners have been slow to recognize recent changes in the way in which health, education and development are understood, and have frequently failed to acknowledge the social and environmental constraints to effective health development. In many schools health education still consists of a few lessons on hygiene, sanitation and nutrition within the science or the domestic science curricula. The purpose of these lessons is to disseminate information to the individual child. No attempt is made to respond to the need to find collective solutions to health problems. The low status traditionally accorded to health education within the curricula of most countries has been slightly raised in recent years in response to growing recognition of the link between health status and educational achievement and to major change in development thinking concerning human resource development. An upsurge of political commitment and advocacy for education and for school health is now reflected in the rhetoric of major international development agencies. The British government Department for International Development (DFID) and the World Health Organization (WHO) illustrate such concerns for improved education and health respectively:

> Education is an essential foundation for the process of enabling individuals and countries to realise their potential and make the most of their resources. ... We will adopt a new approach, working together with governments and international donors to develop education sector policy and financial frameworks. The focus will be on the

fundamental elements of an effective education system: access, reten-
tion, and equity. (DFID 1997)

Education for health is a fundamental right of every child. Health is
inextricably linked to educational achievement, quality of life, and
economic productivity. By acquiring health-related knowledge, values,
skills and practices, children can be empowered to pursue a healthy life
and to work as agents of change for the health of their communities.
The goal can be achieved if we have the will. (WHO 1992a: 1)

Interest in school health has led to increased collaborative research.
For example, the Partnership for Child Development was formed in
1992 by WHO, UNDP and the Rockefeller, Edna McConnell Clark
and James S. McDonnell Foundations. Working in partnership with
Ghana, Indonesia, Colombia and other countries, the Partnership is
conducting operational research projects to determine how a package
of interventions (comprising de-worming tablets, micro-nutrient supplements and health education using Child-to-Child ideas) can be
delivered to children through schools most effectively, at the lowest
cost, and within sustainable programmes (Bundy and Hall 1992;
WHO 1996).

Since 1992 WHO has been developing a comprehensive model
and guidelines for implementing school health programmes. The first
ever WHO Expert Committee Meeting on Comprehensive School
Health Education and Promotion was held in 1995 to launch the
Global School Health Initiative, which promotes the concept of the
health-promoting school in order 'to enable schools to use their full
potential to improve health' (WHO 1996: preface). In recent years we
can see a central role being defined for Child-to-Child ideas and
methods within the concept of the health-promoting school, and the
Trust has made a useful contribution to the literature in publishing
Health Promotion in Our Schools (Hawes 1997), which is a very acces-
sible, practical guide for planners of school health programmes.

Effective strategies for improving health through schooling need to
take into account the fact that in many countries school systems are
already in crisis, curricula are overloaded, resources are diminishing,
school enrolments are increasing and social and economic conditions
limit the impact of schooling in reducing social and economic ills.
Effective health education must be well planned but planners,

especially in developing countries, often cannot access the detailed and credible information needed to apply robust planning frameworks such as that developed by Green and Kreuter (1991). Past failures in health education underscore the need for a systematic approach to programme planning that acknowledges the many constraints to behaviour change. The key to local adaptation is a detailed and sensitive understanding of the social and environmental context. This point is eloquently expressed by Francis:

> Health education should never be seen as the turning of a single key – rather, it involves finding out about the nature of a wide variety of locks and knowing how to make appropriate keys. ... While we may know something about the keys, we are unsure of the nature of the locks in different social and cultural settings. (1993: 19)

We need to identify and involve talented 'locksmiths' who understand the nature of the locks and know how to work sensitively with families and communities to improve health as a key to well-being. Child-to-Child believes that children, together with their teachers, can be these 'locksmiths'. In later chapters of this book we shall be looking at Child-to-Child case studies from different countries to help us to understand better how children can become these 'locksmiths'.

Assessing the Effectiveness of Child-to-Child

In common with other innovations in health promotion, Child-to-Child is still struggling for legitimacy. The flexibility and adaptability of the approach has resulted in great diversity of practice, and until the mid-1990s little systematic attempt had been made to analyse what could be accomplished by the approach. There are many reasons for the paucity of credible evaluation data, not only for Child-to-Child but for school health education and promotion programmes in general. Difficulties arise from the complexity of the communication processes involved, from the need to allow for social and environmental factors and from the confounding influence of other interventions that also impact on health. Moreover, many of the benefits of health education are long-term and may not be measurable for a whole generation. Consequently we can rarely show a direct causal link between a programme and a change in health status. We tend to focus instead on evaluations of intermediate changes in knowledge, attitudes, behaviour or self-empowerment. The problems of evaluating health education programmes are briefly reviewed by Downie et al. (1990: 75–82) and more extensively by Tones et al. (1990: 44–79) and by Green and Kreuter (1991: 79).

During the 1980s the Child-to-Child Trust commissioned two evaluations that charted the spread of the ideas as they were rapidly taken up around the world. The first (Feuerstein 1981) was based on a questionnaire survey and provided useful descriptive data on the various styles of implementation. It recommended that more studies should be conducted to examine the role of the teacher in the Child-to-Child process. The second (Somerset 1987) also used a postal questionnaire survey but supplemented this by visits to three country projects. This survey included 114 projects in 39 countries and produced valuable descriptive data on the activities of the various programmes. It concluded that Child-to-Child had been successful in displacing passive pedagogy, at least during Child-to-Child lessons, and further demonstrated the versatility of the approach in diverse social, cultural and economic situations.

The need to promote research on Child-to-Child was acknowledged by the Child-to-Child Trust in convening a consultative meeting in 1990 to identify important research and evaluation needs and by the subsequent formation of a research subcommittee. This subcommittee commissioned a review of the literature and research on Child-to-Child. The review revealed that the bulk of the research on Child-to-Child consisted of evaluations that do not compare experimental and control groups. Heslop identified a serious gap in the literature: 'None of the papers included in this report provides sufficient information on the social, economic or environmental conditions into which Child-to-Child activities are initiated' (Heslop 1991: 18). A subsequent literature review conducted four years later included a number of small-scale evaluations and four national evaluations but concluded that: 'there have still been no ethnographically based accounts [and] there is a dearth of well controlled studies of the impact of Child-to-Child on health behaviours and status using rigorous design' (Lansdown 1995: 17). Lansdown also noted that little attention had been paid to gender issues.

National evaluations of Child-to-Child activities have been conducted in Uganda, Zambia, India and Botswana. Luswata (1992) examined the Child-to-Child work carried out in Uganda on behalf of UNICEF and found that Child-to-Child was changing the behaviour of children and teachers in participating schools. He concluded that the approach was viable, and argued that with some streamlining of the administration it could be an effective strategy for the country as a whole. Stephens (1998) conducted a controlled study of 247 children in 17 primary schools in and around Kampala examining the impact of a one-year Child-to-Child programme of health education on children's self-concept, behaviour, attendance in school and academic attainment. He found that there were noticeable gains in all the areas for children in the Child-to-Child schools except in the area of academic performance, where there were no significant differences with children in the control schools.

An evaluation of a Child-to-Child project involving 55 primary schools in Zanzibar was conducted by Komba et al. (1997) on behalf of the Aga Khan Foundation. In the absence of any baseline data Komba compared knowledge attitudes and practices in the project schools and their communities with those of a control group. He concluded that the project had enhanced the level of health knowledge and practice in the majority of project communities beyond levels attained by non-Child-to-Child communities, but that there was insufficient evidence to show that the project had made any significant difference to attitudes.

Gibbs (1993, 1997) carried out reviews of the Child-to-Child Programme in Zambia. In the 1993 evaluation he found the number of schools using Child-to-Child was small, with only about 0.01 per cent of children being reached. He concluded that the success of the approach was due to talented and concerned teachers, to supportive head teachers, and to the work of district co-ordinators in spreading the approach. Where Child-to-Child was working at its best he found it had provided an avenue for the professional development of teachers and an active learning environment for children. He noted that Child-to-Child had the opportunity to provide valuable support if health education was to be given a core role in the national curriculum. In the 1997 evaluation he concluded that although Child-to-Child had not proved to be an effective means of delivering health education to all children in primary schools, there were two successful and universal strategies that had proved effective in promoting health knowledge in the schools where Child-to-Child was active: Performance Activities and Surveys. He also recommended that models of good practice should be fully documented and publicized.

The evaluation of Child-to-Child activities sponsored by the Aga Khan Foundation in India (Evans 1993) is the most comprehensive evaluation of Child-to-Child projects to date, differing from others in that it presents both process and impact data. The programmes reviewed took place in seven different settings (urban and rural) between 1986 and 1990, and qualitative case studies and quantitative methods of data collection were both used. The evaluation concluded that Child-to-Child was an effective way to bring health messages to children, particularly in schools, and that it was sustainable because it was continuing in all the settings evaluated after evaluation funding had ceased. This evaluation identified a number of factors that were necessary for successful implementation. These factors were staff participation at all levels and stages of decision-making; an agreed definition of what the Child-to-Child approach means; acknowledgement of the gap between what teachers had been doing and what they were required to do within Child-to-Child; flexibility in the application of the approach; administrative support; teacher training and ongoing support; more than one teacher trained in each school; incentives (not necessarily more pay but recognition of what teachers do); support materials; evaluation beginning before the project got underway and the provision of ongoing evaluation and feedback; Child-to-Child topics integrated into the curriculum; topics relevant to the children's situation, a limited number of topics in a given year; a clear link between schools and health centres; messages from children confirmed by other sources.

An earlier evaluation of school-based Child-to-Child programmes in India funded by the Aga Khan Foundation revealed an important gender disparity. Communication to the parents generally meant communication to mothers rather than to fathers. Girls were more likely than boys to be communicators. Communication to the family and to neighbours was also found to be more effective if children were supported by health personnel or teachers. In the same fashion, children had greater credibility as health educators when they worked together in groups rather than singly in the community (Zaveri 1988).

In Botswana the CHILD-to-child Little Teacher Programme in government primary schools was started in 1979 and is co-ordinated by the CHILD-to-child Network of Botswana. This is a non-governmental organization formerly called the CHILD-to-child Foundation. This programme aims to help schoolchildren (known as little teachers) prepare pre-school children (known as pre-schoolers) for school entry. An evaluation commissioned by UNICEF (Babugura et al. 1993) found that poor record-keeping in schools made evaluations from that source difficult but teachers were 'emphatic' that the programme made a positive difference in preparing children for primary schooling. Children who had been little teachers also appeared to have enjoyed the experience. Parents and community groups were not involved as much as had been hoped and ongoing evaluation by the programme implementers had been only partial. Lesson plans developed in 1979 had not been modified in the light of experience. Despite these points, the overall conclusion was positive, indicating that: 'There is ample evidence that this programme has had a substantial impact on the Botswana community ... many of the programme objectives were achieved and the programme has had a non-trivial impact on the Botswana School Community' (1993: 47).

The evaluations of some small-scale Child-to-Child initiatives also offer useful insights, although these studies have been of a more qualitative kind. Two evaluations report that children have been effective in influencing positive change in health attitudes and the knowledge and behaviour of adults (Fryer 1991; Rhode and Sadjinum 1980). An evaluation of the Malvani Child-to-Child 'Little Doctor' Project in India reported an impressive decrease in scabies (Bhalerao 1981), and Joseph (1980) reported a reduction in common skin complaints as a result of a Child-to-Child programme. Factors that have hindered programme success have highlighted the difficulty of children passing messages to adults in societies in which children occupy a position of low status and where knowledge, attitudes and practices are passed down from older to younger members within the family and community (Somerset 1987; Knight et al. 1991). Reports have also emphasized the need for the credibility of children as educators to be formulated from the start, and for the programme to be systematically established and the community prepared for it (CHETNA 1990).

To conclude this brief review of evaluations of Child-to-Child we need to acknowledge the extent to which evaluators of school health education programmes in developing countries face special problems and constraints. Whereas schools may take responsibility for process evaluation, outcome evaluations are expensive and often require expert input in planning and implementation. Where evaluation data do exist they may not be widely disseminated, particularly in countries that lack the necessary channels of communication such as professional journals and resources for conferences. Schools in many developing countries are experiencing high drop-out rates, high mobility of populations and rapid societal change, which increase the difficulty of evaluating a programme's effectiveness. In many developing countries school attainment and drop-out rates are now used as outcome measures for health education programmes. We need to bear these constraints in mind while at the same time increasing our efforts to gather credible evaluation data on Child-to-Child.

The need for critical reviews of Child-to-Child in its many forms will remain, since all educational programmes that intend to bring about lasting change need to be constantly monitored in terms of both process and impact. As we have shown, it is not easy to carry out such reviews. Countries often lack the necessary resources – personnel, money, transport and time. But progress has been made.

I

An Analysis of the Child-to-Child Approach

2

New Paths to Learning and Health

In this chapter we shall review the literature on learning, education and health from the late 1960s to the mid-1990s to provide the theoretical background for understanding the context in which Child-to-Child was originally formulated and subsequently developed. We shall focus on the theories, and models of learning, education and health, that are central to Child-to-Child and develop working definitions of learning, education and health to provide a benchmark against which to compare the way in which these concepts have been interpreted in practice.

Learning

No one theory of learning has yet provided us with all the answers about how people learn, and the long-standing debate among educational psychologists (see for example Rogers 1996: Chapter 5) has failed to lead to complete agreement about the nature of learning processes. However, in Child-to-Child notions of active learning, lifelong learning and peer learning have been given a central role in the development of the approach.

Active learning The importance of recognizing the role of activity in the learning process has long been accepted in primary education and has always been central to Child-to-Child. As early as 1932 White-head warned us to beware of 'inert ideas' received into the mind without being utilized or tested or used in fresh combinations. He argued strongly that 'education with inert ideas is not only useless – it is above all things, harmful' (1932: 1) and advocated a childhood education filled with the joy of discovery. Early examples of the success of active or participatory learning include the work of Maria Montessori's 'self-education' in Italy, John Dewey's 'teamwork' in the USA, A. S. Neill's 'free school' approach at Summerhill in the UK and Paulo Freire's 'conscientization' methods for adult education in Brazil and Chile.

By the end of the 1960s the United Kingdom was seen to be leading the world in implementing progressive activity-orientated learning methods following the recommendations of the Plowden Commission's report in 1967. The importance of active learning is also a recurrent theme in Bruner's cognitive psychology (1961, 1974). Bruner contends that when people actively construct knowledge they do so by relating incoming information to a previously acquired psychological frame of reference. This frame gives meaning and organization to the regularities in experience, and allows the individual to go beyond the information given. Moreover, Bruner argues that this process is intrinsically empowering: 'an important ingredient [of active learning] is a sense of excitement about discovery of regularities of previously unrecognized relations and similarities between ideas with a resulting sense of self-confidence in one's abilities' (1977: 20).

In 1972 the publication of the Faure Report added further impetus to the active learning movement by arguing that the development of meaningful ideas requires both receptive and enquiry-based learning. It called for new teaching methods to encourage children to learn actively and challenged teachers to master new techniques (Faure et al. 1972). The Faure Report was a milestone in education thinking and provided an early catalyst for the development of Child-to-Child. Hugh Hawes, who has played a central role in the development of Child-to-Child, admits to having been profoundly influenced by the thinking encapsulated in this report and has described it as 'one of the most important single documents to have emerged in the past decade' (Hawes 1979: 161). The centrality of active learning to Child-to-Child is clearly reflected in Somerset's (1987) evaluation and is explored further in Chapter 3.

Lifelong learning The Faure Report argued that to keep abreast of
the fast pace of change in society, individuals, communities and
society as a whole need to be actively involved in the learning process
throughout their lives: 'We should ... learn how to build up a
continually evolving body of knowledge all through life – "learn to
be"' (Faure et al. 1972: iv). The need to find ways of developing
whole societies that can learn together to develop new skills and
solve problems was emphasized by the director-general of UNESCO,
Federico Mayer, in his closing address at the 1991 World Conference
on Education for All: 'Discovering how to learn and how to extend
one's knowledge will ultimately become more important than mere
transmission of knowledge.'

Child-to-Child can be firmly located within the framework of
lifelong learning. Ideas that are central to both concepts include the
importance of horizontal integration of learning experiences; vertical
articulation of such experiences over the lifetime of the learner;
flexibility as to where and when learning can take place; the re-
examination of the role of the school as one agent of education
among many; a broadening of the meaning of 'learner' and of
'teacher' and the concept of a 'learning society' in which individuals
choose their own path to learning.

Peer learning Three kinds of learning relationships involving children
can be distinguished in the education literature: peer tutoring, co-
operative learning and peer collaboration (Foot et al. 1990: 8). Peer
relationships are distinguished by equality in terms of equivalence of
age and stage of cognitive development and equivalence of knowledge or skill in the task or problem to be solved. Peer tutoring is
relatively low on equality and high on mutuality, co-operative learning
is high on equality and low on mutuality, and peer collaboration is
high on both. Peer tutoring includes both cross-age and same-age
tutoring relationships, but there is necessarily an inevitable asymmetry
in the knowledge or skills of the children. As far as the tutoring is
concerned the tutor is the expert and the tutee is the novice.

In collaborative learning children work together to discover solutions and create knowledge by sharing, discussing and challenging
their own partial and incomplete perspectives on a problem. Such

learning implies a relatively symmetrical relationship between the children in an atmosphere of mutual respect and trust, one in which there is no authority relationship between them. Collaborative learning is supported by Piaget's theories of cognitive growth, which argue that peer interaction provides children with the uniquely constructive feedback on which real cognitive development depends (Piaget 1970). The essence of collaborative learning is that children are introduced to new perspectives on problems by engaging in conversation with peers, having their own ideas challenged, and by being forced to 'decentre' in order to take account of these new perspectives. When children disagree with one another and when they have to come to terms with other perspectives, they experience both social and cognitive conflicts that act as the catalyst by which a clearer understanding of the problem emerges.

The term co-operative learning (small group learning) is used to describe situations that are also based upon an essentially symmetrical relationship between interacting children within a classroom. It is an extension of peer collaboration rather than a distinctly different technique. Co-operative learning is relatively structured in that curriculum problems are often segmented into different components and the children take specified and complementary roles.

Theories of peer group learning pose a strong challenge to traditional educational values and practices because they imply radical changes to teacher education, teacher–pupil relationships and classroom management. The teacher has to become a facilitator who is sensitive to the learning needs of the pupils, helps them to work together as a group and encourages the development of critical thinking, problem-solving and decision-making skills. Despite the lip-service paid to co-operative techniques and their well-documented effectiveness in many teaching situations, they are viewed with distrust by many teachers, pupils and parents. We need to break down considerable attitudinal barriers if the enormous potential children have for learning from one another is to be realized. As an alternative approach to teaching and learning Child-to-Child can help us to break down these barriers by demanding that teachers adopt a new way of working with children that involves them in active learning. Many educators now recognize Child-to-Child as a means of bringing active learning into schools that use traditional methods 'through the back door' (Phinney and Evans 1992/3).

Peer group learning is reflected in the original formulation of Child-to-Child, which advocated older children teaching and helping younger children. Although some Child-to-Child initiatives (such as the Little Teacher Programme in Botswana) have continued to use the peer-tutoring model, the current model of Child-to-Child places greater emphasis on collaborative learning.

Micro-cultures of learning An innovative model of learning, put forward by Little (1992), depicts learning as a process of enculturation in which the child is initiated into the culture of the school. Learning occurs when the gap between what the novice (pupil) and expert (teacher) each bring to the so-called 'learning arena' is bridged. This gap results from a combination of differences in knowledge, learning methods, reasons for learning and outcomes of learning. Once the gap is bridged the novice carries a revised set of learning 'equipment' that provides a new baseline from which to start the learning process once more. The nature of the interactions between novices and experts has a powerful influence on future learning because this revised set of 'equipment' may facilitate or hinder future learning, depending on the way in which the learning gap was previously bridged. This is important because it means that if we have good learning experiences we go on to learn better the next time, but if we have bad experiences we are less able to learn next time.

Education

Theories of education tend to overlook theories of learning and to concentrate on broad educational goals. These goals can be very diverse because different models of education envisage strikingly different roles for the school. We need to consider some of these models in order to locate Child-to-Child within a broad framework of educational approaches.

Collective education The collective model of education contends that the individual is to be educated in and by society in order to become a good member of society and work for the good of that society. Consequently children must spend their childhood preparing to become responsible citizens and productive workers. This model raises serious questions of principle and of practice. A well-known example of collective education is the Israeli kibbutz system, but large-scale collective education has been widely adopted around the world in countries with greatly varying political philosophies such as Russia, the former Soviet bloc countries, China and many African states. In certain respects it can also be said to take place in Japan. A detailed account of the expression of theories of collective education in these countries is provided by Sutherland (1988), who concludes that there is insufficient evidence in the literature to assess the extent to which these theories are fully implemented and how much success they have had. Child-to-Child promotes children as good citizens with both rights and responsibilities for health.

Child-centred education Child-centred models of education stress that education in childhood should be a time of happiness when children have freedom to develop their inborn abilities and follow their own interests. The right of children to make decisions for themselves is respected, and the aim of education is to develop the full potential of the individual. Such theories are reflected in progressive educational approaches that emphasise 'play-way' methods, foster self-expression and allow children to choose what to study and what to do. The development of Child-to-Child has been strongly influenced by this model of education and therefore we need to examine it further.

The origins of child-centred education are generally attributed to the writings of Jean-Jacques Rousseau. In his seminal book *Emile* (1762) he rejected traditional views that human beings are naturally wicked and argued that children should be given the freedom to develop naturally through physical activities and real experiences, without having their activities limited by adult prejudices, adult rules and adult choices of subjects to be learned. He believed that such child-centred education would produce a good human being who has enjoyed learning, is keen to continue to learn and is a responsible member of society. Rousseau considered that the role of the educator was to find interesting activities to suit the child at different ages. He identified four main stages of childhood development similar to those made popular in more recent times by Jean Piaget (1970).

Rousseau's original theories have been adapted and extended by other child-centred authorities such as Friedrich Froebel (1782–1852), who emphasized the importance of children's play as the natural way in which children learn about the world. He believed that through play children are free to express their own ideas. He used the metaphor of the kindergarten (garden of children) to suggest that educators, like gardeners, must provide a suitable environment (with toys and games) and protect against damage, but then have faith that growth and blossoming will come from within the child (Froebel 1985).

Educationists have since debated what was meant by the notion of 'natural' development because it is evident that much depends on the environment in which the individual grows. A problem arises in interpreting what is 'natural' in human development in relation to social behaviour. Rousseau rejected the use of adult displeasure or anger to discipline children but contemporary child-centred educators have challenged this view, arguing that it is reasonable for an adult to withdraw affection in response to unacceptable behaviour and that disapproval expressed by the peer group is a 'natural' and highly effective consequence. Moreover, some child-centred educators have deliberately used group pressure (particularly peer group pressure) as a sanction against anti-social behaviour. For example, A. S. Neill's school, Summerhill, developed the system of general meetings in which anyone could bring a complaint against the behaviour of any other individual in the school community (teachers included) and penalties were imposed by the community (Croall 1983).

Child-centred approaches to education such as Child-to-Child have not only emphasized a new kind of discipline and a new definition of what is to be learned but have also focused on learning by experience. These principles have important implications for pedagogy. It can be argued that something the individual has discovered by initiating activities, observing and interpreting the results is more likely to be remembered than something that is passively learned. Consequently we need to involve children in the observation of objects and events in their natural environment and in discovery learning.

It is possible that child-centred education has had most effect on the work of schools through introducing various 'freedoms'. Where formerly pupils were generally expected to remain silent except when replying to the teacher, pupils in many school systems are now permitted to talk to each other during some activities, provided the conversation is about the subject being discussed. Children are generally more able to move around the classroom and, especially in the early years, are likely to have some freedom to choose which activities to engage in.

Child-centred approaches to education also demand a radical reinterpretation of the teacher's role. Traditionally the teacher has been seen as the expert possessing knowledge that is passed to the child. Child-centred education views the teacher as a facilitator, supplying resources the child may need in the process of following natural interest and learning by discovery. The teacher may join with the learner as a partner in a co-operative exploration of materials and situations. Maria Montessori (1918a, 1918b) advocated teachers as resource persons, her method providing an early demonstration that young children can learn a great deal if given suitable learning materials and allowed to use them freely. However, this method has been criticized by child-centred educators because the teacher decides what resources to provide and the child is therefore not entirely free to pursue his or her own interests.

Critics of the child-centred approach have questioned the value of children not receiving adult guidance and pointed out that the naive observer may benefit from expert help to see what is important. They have argued that the teacher should be allowed to intervene if necessary to protect the weaker members of the peer group. In practice a balance is generally struck between the children's freedom to decide what to learn and the teacher's role as facilitator and supporter of that learning. We also need to recognize the way in which cultural values impact on adult–child relationships in the classroom. For example, in many African societies the child-centred approach goes against the strong tradition of children respecting and learning from, rather than with, their elders.

At present we do not have sufficient empirical evidence to show whether the child-centred theory of education is effective. Child-centred education aims to help the individual to learn what is useful and valuable to the individual, to develop the individual's ability to learn independently, to enjoy learning and to continue learning throughout life. Difficulties in evaluation arise because these aims are difficult to measure. Commonly used indicators such as exam success would not be adequate. New indicators would be needed to assess individual happiness (or otherwise) and behaviour towards other people. These difficulties also contribute to the paucity of credible evaluation data on which to assess the effectiveness of Child-to-Child.

We can also question the extent to which child-centred education has really been put into practice. Many teachers assume that by allowing children to move about the classroom, to choose where they will sit and to talk to each other, they are practising some sort of child-centred education, even though other parts of the schoolwork may well be strongly traditional. This reflects a fundamental misinterpretation of the main principles and also the strength of existing practices. Given the difficulties of assessing the effectiveness of child-centred education it may be more useful to consider whether education would be improved by greater use of child-centred methods.

Deschooling Some notable attempts have been made by child-centred educators to free children from the compulsions of schooling. In A. S. Neill's school, Summerhill, lessons are not compulsory. If pupils prefer to spend their time in some other way then they are free to do so.

A more radical solution to the compulsions of schooling was promoted during the 1970s, when a movement emerged that aimed to abolish schools and replace them with radically alternative kinds of education. A drastic attack on the dominance of the school system was made by Ivan Illich (1973) and others who challenged the relevance of schooling to more broadly based human development, and the dominance of the school system in relation to other learning resources such as the family, the peer group or the wider community. During the 1980s Child-to-Child ideas and methods were most quickly taken up and used in non-formal educational settings.

The middle path We can view Dewey's (1964) theory of education as taking a middle position between the strikingly different roles envisaged for the school within child-centred and collective theories of education. Dewey's major contribution was to emphasize the role of the school as an agent of socialization, albeit within a democratic state. He believed that the prime aim of the school was to prepare the individual to live in society through practical experience gained in that society. Consequently he argued that schools should have a special relationship with the community in which they were located. Furthermore, he argued that subjects had merit only if they were of interest to the learner and useful in attaining the learner's own purpose. His ideas led to the development of the Project Method. Later in the book we shall see that Child-to-Child also recognizes the importance of schools building a special relationship with their local communities and developing curricula for health that are interesting and useful to the child.

Empowerment education   In 1968 Paulo Freire published his seminal work, *Pedagogy of the Oppressed*, in which he condemned the passive learning of facts (the so-called 'banking' approach) as an instrument of oppression. He claimed that an approach that challenged learners to struggle with ideas and find solutions to the problems they faced in everyday life could be an instrument of 'conscientization' and consequently of liberation. He stressed that 'conscientization', by which he meant the raising of critical awareness, 'results from search, from the effort to create and re-invent' (Freire 1972: 38).

Freire developed these ideas in the context of adult education and liberation from oppression and recently restated his beliefs, defending their value in progressive education today (Freire 1997). Many of his ideas have been taken up during the 1990s by development agencies interested in child education (such as UNICEF and the Child-to-Child Trust) to promote 'child power'. Critics of these ideas argue that children need guidance and not empowerment. The proponents argue, however, that children have the extraordinary and unique power to act as agents of change within their families and communities and should be helped to do so. They view empowerment as a process of capability-building in children, but stress that children should never be placed in a position where they are openly confronting the values

Figure 2.1 Summary of the major educational influences on Child-to-Child

of their parents or community. We shall explore different interpretations of 'child power' in Chapter 4.

The World Conference on Education for All (WCEFA 1990) identified Basic Education as the means of achieving the global goal of 'Education for All'. Basic Education refers to the child's first contact with the formal school system. The conference advocated increased effort to ensure that schooling resulted in learning, to improve the quality and relevance of education and to reduce the very high dropout rates currently being experienced by many school systems around the world. The Declaration on Education for All raises important questions about how quality and relevance can be fairly assessed in a way that acknowledges the role of culture in the learning process. It recognizes the need to strengthen political support and safeguard a people's right to learn about important aspects of human culture and experience. This was an acknowledgement of the highly political nature of education and the way in which it is a tool of enculturation.

A summary of the major theories of education which have influenced the development of Child-to-Child is given in Figure 2.1.

These ideas about learning and education can now be used as benchmarks in looking at the practice of learning and education. It is universally accepted that the purpose of education is to promote learning. Learning focuses on the psychological processes, which take place within the broader context of education. The following definitions build on a definition by Oxenham (1991: 9) and aim to reflect both the distinction and the interrelationship between learning and education:

Learning is a complex social and psychological process by which we use all our senses, experience, memory and intelligence to acquire much behaviour, many habits and customs, all values, attitudes, knowledge and skills, both mental and muscular. It also comprises the processes by which we modify, refine, extend or develop what we know or can do.

Education is the empowerment of individuals through the provision of learning. It is the whole sum of a person's learning and what promotes or has promoted it, which enables him or her to think, and to use knowledge in order to survive and to become a fully developed member of society. Education is truly a human right and a responsibility.

These definitions reflect broad-based, multidimensional models of learning and education that cut across boundaries of discipline and culture. They acknowledge that social as well as psychological factors influence learning and education, and acknowledge the interaction of stimuli from the body's senses with experience and intelligence. They also encompass the basic premise that learning is the core activity of education and occurs whenever one adopts new or modifies existing knowledge or behaviour patterns.

Health

It is difficult for us to define any universally acceptable conceptualization of health. Health is interpreted in very diverse ways by the different populations of the world, and understanding of health is always evolving. For example, at the beginning of the twentieth century in England, as a result of secularization, earlier notions of health being determined by God were replaced by ideas of health resulting from natural causes. By the 1960s an interactive model had emerged in which the individual had some ability to act. By the late 1980s and 1990s an intra-active model had evolved in which the individual is able to act upon himself or herself by adopting a healthy lifestyle.

It is important for us to recognize that these different interpretations of health have led to different solutions to health problems. The notion of health as being the possession of an individual rather than a group needs to be questioned in view of the increased recognition now given to the importance of social, cultural and environmental influences on health (see for example Caldwell 1993). We can most usefully analyse the various approaches to health by considering the different socio-political philosophies that inform them. For instance, we can argue that a biomedical or curative approach to health is informed by a deficit model in which individual inadequacies require correction; an ecological approach is informed by a deprivation model in which social injustices require resource redistribution; and a more radical pluralist approach is informed by an emancipation model requiring community mobilization and direct action. The value of a socio-political analysis of approaches to health has been recognized by Beattie et al. (1993: 264) in developing their innovative series of models of health. It will be useful for us to look more closely at those concepts of health that have helped to shape Child-to-Child.

The WHO definition of health was first presented in the 1946 Constitution of the World Health Organization and is still widely quoted. Health is defined as 'a state of complete physical, mental and social well-being, and not merely the absence of disease or infirmity (WHO 1984: 1). This definition has been criticized, however, for being Utopian. A complete state of well-being is idealistic and unattainable and therefore of little relevance to the lives of most individuals. Moreover, representing health as a static state does not acknowledge its relative and dynamic nature or allow for improvement. Despite these criticisms, the WHO definition has merit in recognizing health as more than the absence of disease and acknowledging three of its dimensions. It promotes health as a state of well-being, a notion that is currently enjoying popularity (Beattie et al. 1993).

Health has frequently been interpreted as a state of harmony and balance. We can often trace the origins of popular concepts of health back to the thinking of early Greek philosophers such as Hippocrates, whose doctrine of 'universal sympathy' or harmony viewed health as a state of balance or equilibrium between the internal and external environments of an individual. The external environment was considered to comprise the four elements of earth, air, fire and water. These notions are important because they are still reflected in the beliefs of many traditional societies and ancient religions, for whom health involves living at peace with oneself and one's ancestors and with the wider spiritual world. Most societies harbour the nebulous myth of a bygone 'Golden Era' that symbolizes a time when people were essentially 'good' and lived in an ideal state of harmony among themselves and with nature. René Dubos drew on Rousseau's famous idealization of 'the noble savage' to support his argument that health is just a mirage that is central to man's striving to regain paradise on earth through a return to nature:

> Man in his original state was good, healthy and happy and all his troubles came from the fact that civilisation had spoiled him physically and corrupted him mentally ... 'Hygiene' is less a science than a virtue. 'Sickness' being the result of straying away from the natural environment, the blessed original state of health and happiness could be recaptured only through abiding by the simple order and purity of nature. (1979: 106)

This deep-rooted belief that ill health is a result of man's failure to achieve harmony with nature is still dominant in traditional agrarian societies that live closely with nature. It is also currently enjoying something of a renaissance in the developed world, where it is attractive to the environmental lobby. The notion of health as universal harmony and balance is reflected in the texts and practices of Ayurvedic (herbalist) medicine, established throughout the Indian subcontinent. This view of health is one of the most widely held in the world today.

Health may also be viewed as the absence of disease. The alternative conceptualization of health, informed by the doctrine of specific aetiology, links disease with a precise cause derived from the medical sciences. This conceptualization has resulted in the progressive medicalization of health in Western countries over the twentieth century and has led to the development of a so-called 'medical model' of health. This model equates good health with the provision of effective medical services to cure disease and regards the human body as a machine that is protected from disease primarily by external interventions. Unfortunately, this model has been exported to poor countries around the world and has resulted in scarce resources being channelled into building hospitals to provide expert curative care for the few, which has left the health needs of the many largely unmet. To highlight the social injustice of this action, Morley and Lovel (1986: 64) refer to hospitals as 'disease palaces'. Recognition of the inability of the medical model to prevent increasing inequalities in health has resulted in a global backlash against the medicalization of health. This backlash has also been fuelled by the radical critique of contemporary medicine, which grew up in the 1970s through the writings of Cochran (1971), Illich (1976), McKeown (1976, 1979) and others.

Illich's (1976) emotive and much quoted discourse on 'The epidemics of modern medicine' argues that medicine is essentially sinister and produces so-called 'iatrogenic' diseases. Such diseases are caused directly by medical treatment and result in 'medical nemesis' by producing a self-reinforcing loop of negative institutional feedback. According to Illich, medicine is a direct threat to health because it removes the right of individuals to take control of their own lives and to deal with their own health problems. This debate has been taken further by McKeown (1979) in his seminal thesis *The Role of Medicine: Dream, Mirage or Nemesis?*, which argues that external influences and personal behaviour are the predominant determinants of health. There is now a substantial body of empirical evidence to show that although medical care has saved the lives of countless individuals it has contributed little to improving the health of nations. We shall see later in this chapter that the key to further improvement in health is now acknowledged to involve change in the social, cultural and behavioural determinants of health (Caldwell 1993).

We can now develop a working definition of health. There are many useful definitions of health in the literature (Dubos 1979; WHO 1984; Kickbush 1986), but no universal definition has yet been agreed. The definition needs to be positive, multidimensional (holistic), acceptable to many cultures, able to surmount the constraints of different disciplinary boundaries and able to avoid the problematic notion of health as the sole possession of an individual. Bearing these criteria in mind we have developed the following definition:

> Health is a resource for life. It is a relative and positive concept emphasizing social, mental, emotional and spiritual well-being as well as physical capacities. It is the extent to which an individual or group is

able to realize aspirations, satisfy needs and adapt to change in the environment.

This definition sees health as having no purpose of its own but only as a vehicle for living. It reflects a broad conceptualization of health that acknowledges its positive, relative and changing nature as well as its multiple causality. It emphasizes social and personal resources as well as physical capacities, and acknowledges the importance of being able to adapt to change. It also allows for a collective as well as an individual dimension. We shall see that there is considerable variation in the concept of health that informs Child-to-Child in the different case studies presented later in the book.

Health Education

Health education has only recently emerged as a discipline in its own right. It has been criticized for lacking any universally accepted philosophy, clear goals or unifying framework of theory and also because in practice it reflects a diverse range of processes. The substantial ideological differences that exist between the approaches being used have produced much divisive debate, Volume 49 (1990) of the *Health Education Journal* being entirely devoted to this debate.

Let us now move on to consider models of health education. Health educators have been much concerned with developing working models to explain particular health education initiatives. This approach contrasts with that found in the more established disciplines of health and education, where theoretical models are generally designed to help clarify and develop concepts and facilitate the testing of theory against practice. According to Rawson (1992: 206–12) there are now well over a hundred health education models to choose from, and numerous taxonomies. The proliferation of models has generated a substantial literature (Ewles and Simnett 1985; French and Adams 1986; Downie et al. 1990; Tones et al. 1990; Macdonald 1993; Baric 1995).

We can distinguish three dominant models: preventive, social action and self-empowerment.

In the preventive model the goal of the health educator is to persuade the individual to adopt positive health behaviours and so prevent disease. Tones et al. (1990) argue that this model is endowed with conservative and paternalistic values and reflects an approach to health education commonly known as the 'healthy lifestyles' approach. Health education informed by this model can be criticized as unethical because its goal is to change behaviour by fair means or foul (philosophically speaking). It can also lead to 'victim blaming' by ignoring social and environmental determinants of health.

In the more radical-political models the educator aims to raise critical consciousness and empower community groups to take social action to reduce structural barriers to health improvement.

In the self-empowerment model the educator provides information and helps clarify values underlying decision-making, but does not persuade. This model stresses the need for informed consent in contrast to models of propaganda, persuasion, instruction and even training that give no thought to the moral outcome of learning.

Preventive, social action and self-empowerment models represent fundamental dichotomies within the theory of health education. The self-empowerment model, for example, is ideologically opposed to the preventive model. In practice, however, the ideological differences between the different models of health education are often reconciled. Moreover, the simultaneous application of multiple theories and models is not only desirable but also necessary for effective health education:

> No single theory is sufficient to guide the development, operation, and management of an effective health education programme. Decisions about appropriate methodology, strategic application, management, and evaluation are almost always based on the complementary application of social, behavioural, educational, biomedical, and organisational models for change. (Dhillon and Tolsma 1992: 7)

Child-to-Child is informed largely by the preventive and self-empowerment models of health education. Child-to-Child aims to build children's capabilities to take preventive health action. The approach also recognizes that children have an extraordinary and unique power to act as agents of social change within their communities and argues that they should be helped to do so.

Drawing on definitions by Downie et al. (1990: 28) and by Dhillon and Tolsma (1992: 8) we can now develop a working definition of health education:

> Health education is communication activity involving planned social actions and learning experiences designed to enable people to gain control over the determinants of health behaviours and the conditions that affect their health status and the health status of others. The aim of health education is to enhance positive health and prevent or diminish ill health in individuals and groups.

This definition emphasizes the need for health education to be a planned process and it allows for the application of conflicting educational theories and models. In stressing that the aim of health education is to enable people to gain control over the determinants of health behaviours it promotes self-empowerment and recognizes the influence of what Green and Kreuter (1991) have called predisposing, enabling and reinforcing factors. It also recognizes the need to work with policy-makers, communities and individuals. The definition of health education that informs Child-to-Child conforms well to our working definition. Child-to-Child promotes a methodology that aims to involve children in active learning, to build their capabilities for health action, and to promote collaboration at all levels of those involved in improving health.

Health Promotion

In recent years health education has been located within the overarching concept of health promotion, which recognizes the need to support health education through building healthy public policy and creating supportive environments for health. The health promotion movement gathered momentum during the 1980s in response to increasing awareness of the ecological reality of health and of the political dimensions of disease and health care. The publication of the *Ottawa Charter for Health Promotion* (WHO 1986) provided a valuable framework for programme development, and officially launched a new public health movement based on health promotion. WHO views health promotion as an over-arching and unifying concept that builds on the earlier philosophy of Primary Health Care (PHC) encapsulated in the Alma Ata Declaration (WHO 1978). This earlier Declaration was the milestone in health development thinking and highlighted growing inequities in health. It was informed by a holistic concept of health, promoted inter-sectoral collaboration and enjoined all community members to take interest and action to preserve their own health and the health of fellow human beings. It emphasized people's right to health knowledge and skills and promoted prevention before cure. It questioned the medico-technical intervention model of health, and challenged the professional interests vested in the traditional system of medical care by advocating the reorientation of health services to shift resources away from hospitals and into community health activities. The PHC approach to health education places considerable emphasis on building people's confidence in their ability to take individual and collective action to improve health. It also advocates what Macdonald (1993: 145) has referred to as 'life-context' education that recognizes the need to take account of the social and environmental context within which behaviour change takes place.

WHO has defined health promotion as 'the process of enabling people to increase control over, and to improve, their health' (1986: 1). The key word 'enabling' underscores the need for a shift in power over health from bureaucracies to people, and recognizes that power and control are the central issues in health promotion, just as they are in Primary Health Care. This definition also acknowledges the collective nature of health improvement and reinforces the argument presented above that an individual notion of health is problematic because people cannot be seen in social isolation. Individuals are embedded in systems that profoundly affect their behaviour and their health. To improve health, communities need to gain more control over these systems through their full involvement in decision-making processes.

As the health promotion movement has grown, the concept of health promotion has been interpreted in increasingly diverse ways (Anderson 1984; Baric 1985; Green and Raeburn 1988; Downie et al. 1990; Kickbush 1990). However, within the literature three main themes can be distinguished which contribute to health promotion: education, prevention and protection. Health education (as defined in our working definition) involves planned social actions and learning experiences to enable people to gain control over the determinants of health. WHO has coined the phrase 'education for health' to advocate this conceptualization of health education and it is being promoted as a key strategy for achieving the global goal of 'Health for All'. Health prevention involves the adoption of so-called 'healthy lifestyles' and the uptake of preventive health services such as childhood immunization. Health protection refers to legal and fiscal measures to protect health.

The role of health education within health promotion is summarized in Figure 2.2. Education contributes to health through preventive health education, professional education and agenda-setting. Preventive health education traditionally includes efforts to influence individuals and groups to adopt healthy habits. Professional education involves health educators working with professionals from the health and health-related disciplines to develop communication skills and to encourage them to take greater responsibility for health promotion. In this role the health educator also aims to facilitate the delivery of primary health services that meet real community needs.

Agenda-setting promotes social action designed to raise public awareness and put pressure on policy-makers and politicians to implement policies that they may otherwise fail to implement on financial or ideological grounds. Agenda-setting is informed by the Freirean notion of 'praxis', which involves individuals and groups reflecting critically on their lives and the environment in which they live and then taking action to improve the quality of their lives.

Community action includes individuals and community groups in social encounters that require good communication skills for effective advocacy, lobbying and mediation. Examples of public health policies in the UK include fluoridation of water, restrictions on tobacco advertising and legislation on wearing car seat-belts. Examples from Botswana include food safety and hygiene legislation, the use of safe water supplies, regulation of the price of staple foodstuffs and the wearing of hard hats on motorbikes.

We can now develop a definition of health promotion. The following working definition draws on a definition by Tones et al. (1990: 4):

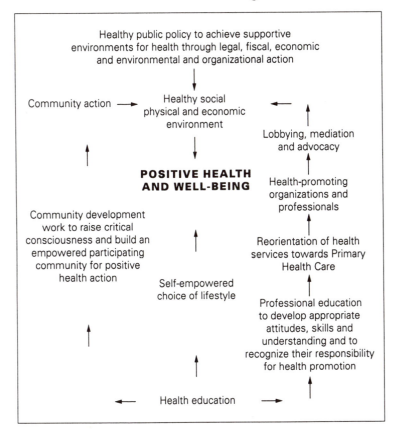

Healthy public policy to achieve supportive
environments for health through legal, fiscal, economic
and environmental and organizational action

Community action ⟶ Healthy social
physical and economic
environment

Lobbying, mediation
and advocacy

**POSITIVE HEALTH
AND WELL-BEING**

Health-promoting
organizations and
professionals

Community development
work to raise critical
consciousness and build an
empowered participating
community for positive
health action

Reorientation of health
services towards Primary
Health Care

Self-empowered
choice of lifestyle

Professional education
to develop appropriate
attitudes, skills and
understanding and to
recognize their responsibility
for health promotion

⟵ Health education ⟶

Figure 2.2 A model of health promotion showing the role of health
education (*source*: adapted from Tones et al. 1990: 3).

Health promotion is any combination of education and related legal,
fiscal, economic, environmental and organizational interventions
designed to facilitate the achievement of positive health and well-being
and the prevention of ill health.

This definition recognizes the underlying determinants of health. It
includes the three main components of health promotion – education,
prevention and protection – and reflects a positive conceptualization
of health.

Child-to-Child as a 'bag' of ideas and methods has come a long way since its inception in 1979. During that journey it has been influenced by prevailing influences within the fields of health and education. Its relationship to development is an important one, and is taken up in the next chapter.

3

Education and Health for Development

In this chapter we shall address the complex interrelationships between education, health and development to increase understanding of the context in which Child-to-Child was originally formulated and in which it has subsequently developed. The literature will be analysed to explore the two assumptions on which Child-to-Child rests: that education can improve health and that healthy children learn better at school. We shall argue that there is much evidence to support these assumptions, and that efforts to improve health and education work together as so-called 'energizers' of development.

Development

In recent years a significant change in thinking about how development occurs has amounted to a paradigm shift. We no longer regard either economic growth or the redistribution of wealth as an adequate single measure of the development process. The focus now is on human resource development (HRD) and on working with people's own ideas of what development means to them. Human resource development is measured by a scale called the Human Development Index (HDI). HRD takes account of the growth and liberation of people and accords a central role to education and health as a means of improving the quality of life. It takes into account the importance of ethical and spiritual values and stresses the need to enable the poor to become active participants in solving their own problems and in shaping their own destiny. HRD is now promoted by all major international development agencies (WHO 1988; UNDP 1990).

A working definition of development has been developed to reflect the new ideas about development. It draws on a definition by the UNDP (1990):

> Development is about enlarging the choices which people can make. This involves the growth of people as well as income, the quality of life, the participation of people in their own development and human freedom. Neither economic growth nor the redistribution of income can be construed as ends in themselves; both serve human development as much as human development serves them and education serves all three.

This definition acknowledges the importance of increasing people's choices, of which a long and healthy life, the acquisition of knowledge and access to a decent standard of living are arguably priorities. It also recognizes important synergies between human resource development and political and economic freedom. Investment in schooling and health, together with economic policies to alleviate poverty and efforts to promote the rights and status of women, are now considered to be the keys for transforming vicious cycles of poverty, malnutrition, disease and ignorance into 'virtuous cycles' of learning and health, equity and sustainable development (World Bank 1993).

Education and Development

Education lays the foundation for development, being critical to both economic growth and human development. However, the relationship is not a simple one of cause and effect. History has shown that education alone is unable to produce the desired development and although education is currently enjoying a central role in the development process, it has not always been regarded so highly. Reflecting on the fluctuating fortunes of education in recent times, Little (1992: 1) has commented humorously that 'education, the-innocent-turned-villain, is cast once again by the international development planners in a positive role whose character is tinged with that of the saviour rescuing us from our perils'.

Human capital theory (Schultz 1961) has preoccupied economists and strongly influenced thinking in education and development since the 1960s. Modernization theory has also been influential, especially among sociologists (McClelland 1961; Anderson and Bowman 1966; Inkeles and Smith 1974). Both of these theories are severely criticized, however, by those who reject capitalist-orientated society and view education as an important tool in the reproduction of inequalities within society. The thinking of these theorists is informed by the reactive theories of Marxism (Bowles and Gintis 1976; Fagerlind and Saha 1989), neo-Marxism (Illich 1973; Apple 1982) and dependency theory (Carnoy 1974). The extensive literature on education and development can be accessed through two comprehensive overviews of theories and concepts (Fagerlind and Saha 1989; Little and Yates 1991). Evidence for the effects of education on development objectives is the focus of a review by Lewin (1993) in which he draws on two earlier papers by Lewin et al. (1983a, 1983b).

As we approach the end of the 1990s, it is possible to identify seven major quality issues in education and development:

1. the structure and organization of the education system, e.g. issues of access, diversification;
2. the financing and resourcing of the schools, e.g. targeting aid to lower levels of the system, issues of community financing;
3. questions of curriculum development and assessment, e.g. issues of balance between the academic and vocational;
4. matters of teacher training and support, e.g. a movement away from pre- to in-service training;
5. management, administration and planning, e.g. issues of decentralization and over-bureaucratization;
6. community–school relations, e.g. issues of relevance and accountability; and
7. issues of the paucity of research and understanding of what is actually happening in our classrooms.

Child-to-Child is particularly concerned with issues of curriculum, teacher support and school–community relations. There is strong support for the view that Child-to-Child can take a lead in encouraging school-based research, particularly of an action-oriented kind (Stephens 1996).

Proactive theories of education and development   After the Second World War education was grasped as a means of producing the 'human capital' needed to fuel economic growth and recovery in Europe. Human capital refers to the volume and productivity of human labour within a nation. Human capital theory has been clearly articulated by Schultz (1961, 1971), who argues for investment in education on the grounds that an educated population provides the type of labour force needed to improve human capital. This theory is supported by evidence to show a consistent empirical relationship between levels of education and economic levels of development among countries. For example, Psacharopoulos (1985) demonstrated that all rates of return on investment in education were above the 10 per cent criterion of the opportunity cost of capital in each of the 44 countries he studied, and that rates of return were higher in less developed countries. Schultz also recognized that investment in 'child capital' could be a key to development:

> The formation of 'child capital' by the household, man and wife would begin with the bearing of children and proceed through their rearing throughout childhood ... and may hold the key to an economic theory of population. (1971: vii)

Human capital theory is currently enjoying increased popularity, even though it was previously criticized for failing to reduce inequalities in societies despite the rapid and massive educational expansion that has taken place in most countries. It ignores the costs of educational systems and the influence of incentives and job satisfaction on labour productivity. It assumes erroneously that those who are better educated necessarily get better jobs and are more productive. Furthermore, the rapid pace of development in Japan and Korea was founded not solely on mass literacy and numeracy but on socio-economic regulation, land reform and modern economic management (Hallak 1990).

Modernization theory was first fully elucidated in 1961 in McClelland's seminal book *The Achieving Society*. This theory argues for a direct causal link between modernizing institutions, modern values, modern behaviour, modern society and economic development. McClelland identifies a personality characteristic in society, called 'achievement motivation', which involves early socialization. He considers it to be the key to accelerating economic growth. McClelland's views are endorsed by later writers such as Inkeles and Smith, who contend that 'it is impossible for a state to move into the twentieth century if its people continue to live in an earlier era' (1974: 4). They view schooling in developing countries as a powerful means of inculcating modern attitudes, values and behaviour.

In response to the acceptance of education as the key to modernization, school enrolment increased impressively during the 1960s. Governments of newly independent countries also grasped education as a means of creating a new national identity, promoting it as a basic human right and changing its established features to forge and safeguard national unity. At this time there was rapid growth in nonformal education. This provided mostly for the poorest children who, for social and economic reasons, could not find a place in the formal system and offered an alternative education for those disillusioned with this system (Hallak 1990).

Modernization theory has been much criticized, although it still informs education planning in many countries. It has been largely discredited because there is insufficient evidence that modern attributes lead to socio-economic development (Portes 1973; Fagerlind and Saha 1989), and modern values have been blamed for the professional 'brain drain' from developing to developed countries (Portes 1973). The way in which modernization has been equated with Westernization has been criticized for displaying a biased and ethnocentric viewpoint, for implying that the traditions of a society are backward and for ignoring the impact of more developed countries on those less developed (Illich 1973). Modernization theory assumes that the traditional and the modern are in competition, yet some of the most successful countries in the developing world have shown that modern attitudes and values are not incompatible with traditional ones. Japan has achieved accelerated economic development by accepting new technological ideas and implementing them within its traditional cultural systems.

Against all predictions, the heavy investment in education and training during the 1950s and 1960s failed to produce the desired development. Economic growth stagnated, rates of unemployment among the educated rose and income disparities increased. Subsequently disillusionment with education set in during the 1970s, and in 1976 Dore elucidated his thesis of 'late development'. He coined the phrase 'the Diploma Disease' to describe the way in which acquiring qualifications ('credentialling') had too often become the be-all and end-all of schooling, as formal qualifications became increasingly important for securing a job. His thesis is a predominantly sociological analysis. It argues that educational quality is partly determined by the way in which the labour market uses educational certificates for recruitment and that this use in turn depends on the time in world history at which the move towards industrial development is started:

> The later development starts the more widely education certificates are used for occupational selection; the faster the rate of qualification inflation and the more exam-orientated schooling becomes at the expense of genuine education. (Dore 1976: 72)

This focus on the acquisition of formal qualifications is clearly most worrying for poor countries where, as Little and Dore (1982) have also recognized, the premium placed on diplomas is highest and where the contribution that schools could make to solving the problems of development is crucial.

By the time disillusionment with formal education set in during the 1970s, an acrimonious debate had developed as to whether formal education is a productive force for change or a reproductive force reinforcing existing inequities within society. This debate has attracted a large and diverse literature (Seers 1969; Ward 1974; Durkheim 1977; Bernstein 1979; Lewin et al. 1983b; Blaug 1985; Borini 1986; Fagerlind and Saha 1989). Those who support investment in formal education draw on proactive theories of education and development to argue that formal education promotes the skills and motivation necessary (though not sufficient) for productive behaviour leading to both economic and social development. Those who argue against investment in formal education draw on reactive Marxist or neo-Marxist theories of education and development that are concerned with structural inequalities within society and argue for radical reform of education.

Reactive theories of education and development According to Marxist theory, education is a form of cultural and economic reproduction. Educational institutions in capitalist-oriented societies are a means of perpetuating the privileged classes and keeping the poor in their place. Capitalist-orientated society is repressive and inhumane. Class-based and individual behaviour is the product of historical forces rooted in material conditions. Conflict within society arises from exploitation by those who own the means of production (the bourgeoisie) of those who do not (the proletariat). Such conflict is accorded a central role in the theory of change. Consequently the Marxist theorists Bowles and Gintis (1976) reject the assumption that development follows a linear or stage-by-stage pattern, and contend that change comes about through revolution.

Recent interpretations of Marx's original position give greater weight in the reproduction process to schooling, because in schooling reproduction takes its most organized form. The radical critiques of writers such as Illich (1973) constitute a strong and persuasive challenge to the education–development hypothesis. Illich's call for 'deschooling' warned that expansion of schooling would aggravate inequalities within less developed countries. Although there is much support in the literature for the view that schools are institutions of economic and cultural reproduction, the process by which this happens is exceptionally complex and not clearly understood (Apple 1982).

Dependency theory, an alternative perspective developed from the orthodox Marxist perspective, rests on the assumption that development and underdevelopment, as relational concepts within and between societies, are inversely related (Fagerlind and Saha 1989). Dependency between the development of central societies and underdevelopment of peripheral or satellite societies is an historical and intentional process. Dependency theory focuses on social, cultural, political and economic processes by which poor countries are dependent on rich countries. It argues that these processes are identical to those whereby the metropolis dominates rural areas within a country. The school models adopted in peripheral countries depend on what is imposed on them from the core country and thus education is seen as perpetuating dependency and cultural imperialism. This theory has been criticized for failing to provide a viable strategy for development, which is free of dependency on rich countries. Furthermore, there is no explanation as to how the elite of a poor country, seen as collaborators of the elites of rich countries, can overcome self-interest in favour of the society as a whole.

Although polarizing the issues around schooling as 'production or reproduction' has produced much lively debate and useful insight, the two extreme perspectives are often assumed to have universal relevance. In fact they reflect a narrow conceptualization of education and development, with development confined to economic growth and education confined to formal schooling. This debate needs to acknowledge the influence of external and internal forces, which act on a nation at specific times in history. Since the collapse of communism in Russia and Eastern Europe it has become evident that, despite their Marxist perspectives, these countries have looked to education to produce the workforce needed for economic development and have experienced many of the problems they had previously attributed to the capitalist system itself (Fagerlind and Saha 1989).

Education for All Since the 1980s faith in education to promote development has been restored. There is a growing consensus in support of increased spending, particularly on basic education. We saw in Chapter 1 that the World Conference on Education for All (WCEFA 1990) hailed primary schools as major social institutions to reduce inequalities and contribute to democracy. This provided a strong mandate for education planners to argue for increased resources from national governments on ethical, economic, social, cultural and ecological grounds. However, Lewin (1993) has found much evidence that the recession, debt and structural adjustment have all impacted to reduce spending on education. In Chapter 4 we will see how Child-to-Child claims to have capitalized on the publicity and the political will for change engendered by the goal of Education for All.

Education and quality and the focus on girls At the World Conference on Education for All, two major issues preoccupied those attending: first, the question of quality of primary education in most parts of the world, and second, the pronounced gender gap in access to, and achievement in, schools in many developing countries.

Questions of quality have been researched and debated in a range of fora and publications (see for example Hawes and Stephens 1990; Lockheed and Verspoor 1991; Stephens 1996), and much of the debate now focuses on the importance of learning outcomes and the development and identification of school effectiveness (Harber and Davies 1997). The issue of gender disparities and more particularly problems of female enrolment and drop-out is equally well researched (see for example Colclough et al. 1998; Stephens 1998). Here the complex relationships of poverty, schooling and gender are to the fore with the debate increasingly taking up the matter of culture seriously. The impact on, and the role of, Child-to-Child in the promotion of quality in education and the targeting of girls particularly as the carriers of health messages has been recognized.

Education and Health

The literature on education and health is small in comparison with that on education and development. However, there is a substantial literature around the effects of education on health status (Cochrane 1979; Cochrane et al. 1982; Lewin et al. 1983b; Blaug 1985; Psacharopoulos 1985). There is also a small, but rapidly expanding, literature on the effects of health status on educability (Pollitt 1984, 1990; Ivanovic 1991; World Bank 1993; Levinger 1994.). A related literature focuses on education, health and the demographic transition (Caldwell 1986; Lewin 1993). The *World Development Report: Investing in Health* (World Bank 1993) is a major contribution to the literature, providing a comprehensive review of evidence to link education and health as so-called 'energizers' of development.

Equity and inter-sectoral collaboration The global goals of Health for All (WHO 1978) and Education for All (WCEFA 1990) were a response to perceived inequities in health and in education. These goals have been endorsed by the World Bank (1993). Calls for reform towards greater equity are supported by strong evidence that efforts to improve health and education are most effective when all members of society receive, at least, basic services (Caldwell 1986). Despite these calls for reform it is still common for the available health and education resources to be spent lavishly caring for or teaching a few. Reform is urgently needed to enable the most vulnerable groups to have first call on limited resources rather than those who are best able to pay.

Despite international rhetoric in support of investment in health care and education, national governments continue to place them at the bottom of the pile in terms of funding allocation. In most developing countries less than 12 per cent of government spending is invested in the health and education of the poor majority (UNICEF 1992: 29). Continued low spending reflects lack of political will to reduce inequalities. Development is also impeded by lack of skill in planning and managing health promotion programmes (Green and Kreuter 1991). Effective programmes need to be multifaceted to reduce poverty, to improve the quality and quantity of foodstuffs and water supplies and to safeguard the environment and women's rights.

The relationship between poverty and educational development is now a major priority for policy-makers (DFID 1997). Christopher Colclough's team of researchers at the Institute of Development Studies at Sussex University has identified four main factors. At the level of the home, the direct costs of schooling are too high and child labour is required to sustain the household, while at the level of the state it is the insufficient number of school places available and the poor quality of education delivered that combine to produce gender inequalities in primary schooling (Colclough et al. 1998).

A major plank in Child-to-Child's development as a charitable trust has been the argument that primary health care is a more profitable and cost-effective way to improve the health of the population. By focusing on the energy and enthusiasm of children as a human resource, it is argued, savings can be made in health budgets and an investment made in reducing future health expenditure on those children when entering adult life.

Co-operation is vital for joint planning and sharing of available resources and also for the development and activation of effective structures to facilitate the co-ordination needed at all levels both within and between organizations. This requires co-ordination between ministries (especially those of education and health); between

ministries and multinational corporations; between NGOs (international, national and local) and government organizations; between
teacher training colleges and health training schools; between these
training institutions, schools and health facilities; between teachers,
parents, students, health workers, local community leaders and
businesses; and between traditional healers, health workers and other
extension workers. We saw in Chapter 1 that Child-to-Child recognized from the start that effective co-ordination between health and
education at all these levels was essential for improving health.

Education and health status The development of Child-to-Child in
the late 1970s was, in part, a response to strengthening evidence of
the importance of investing in education as a means of improving
health. In 1979 Susan Cochrane produced the first of a series of
World Bank Staff Working Papers on education and health, which
reviewed evidence on education and fertility. This paper found that
although education may result in initial rises in fertility, 'in the long
term fertility may be reduced as a result of recognizing the increased
ability to have live births and the survival of those births' (1979: 141).
In general, more educated mothers tended to have smaller families
providing education was sufficiently widely available to reach certain
thresholds of educational level. There is now a considerable body of
evidence to demonstrate that education of females is inversely related
to family size (World Bank 1992; Lewin 1993). It has also been demonstrated that fertility rates are closely related to child survival rates
and to population growth rates, both of which impact on the demand
for educational services.

Recently published data from the 1970 birth cohort study in the
UK appears to show a clear correlation between social inequality and
levels of educational attainment and health. Those who lack educational qualifications are, at age 26 years, four times more likely to
report poor general health than those with the highest qualifications
(Montgomery and Schoon 1997). We now know that households with
more education enjoy better health, both for adults and for children.
This result is strikingly consistent in a great number of studies, despite
differences in research methods, time periods and population samples
(World Bank 1993: 42).

In many studies, however, the level of education acts as a marker for the effects of other influences such as social class, occupational level or lifestyle. Education can play multiple and important roles in preventing death and disease, but the relationships are not simple. A comparative study of health development measured gains in child health in 75 countries with different income levels between 1960 and 1987 (World Bank 1993: 38). The results of this study confirmed that in all countries only part of the gain came from initial levels of schooling in the population and income per capita (both of which produced benefits that persisted over time). Part of the gain came also from expansion of schooling, increases in income per capita and technological progress in science and medicine. However, the relative contribution of these factors differed greatly between countries. Similarly, Wilkinson (1996) draws attention to the cumulative effect of low social class of origin, poor educational achievement, reduced employment prospects, low levels of psycho-social well-being and poor physical and mental health. It therefore appears that education is linked to health through the differential opportunities for income, employment and security associated with different levels of educational attainment. In this way education may both trigger healthier lifestyles and behaviour and protect individuals from disadvantage in later life.

Demographic ageing and the health transition In the long term, improved health is an important factor in the demographic transition countries make from high fertility and high mortality rates to low fertility and low mortality rates in the course of development. Economic decline is currently trapping many developing countries in the so-called population 'transition gap' in which fertility rates remain high but mortality rates are lowered. This unstable state results in rapid population growth that dissipates the products of economic growth and slows development. The demographic transition has important implications for the provision of education (see Lewin 1993) and health services.

As countries develop, infectious diseases are increasingly replaced by chronic diseases such as diabetes and coronary heart disease. This change in the disease pattern associated with development is commonly called the health transition. Evidence that medical interventions can account at most for a difference of 10–15 years in life expectancy (cf. a 40-year difference in life expectancy between countries in the North and the South) has led to much effort to identify other factors involved. These other factors have been identified as cultural, social and behavioural determinants of health.

Caldwell (1986) analysed the process by which good health had been achieved in eleven poor countries where investment in basic education and health services has achieved remarkable national health improvement at low cost. The experiences of China, Costa Rica, Sri Lanka and Kerala state in India are frequently quoted examples. Caldwell found the strongest correlation with health success to be the educational levels of women of maternal age, followed closely by the practice of family planning and the education of men, and more distantly by the density of doctors and nutritional levels. He found a weak correlation with per capita income. Furthermore, his study identified antecedent factors of health success in traditionally more egalitarian and democratic societies, such as high levels of social and economic participation on the part of women and a demand for health services and education, especially the education of girls. These antecedents are long-term assets (social capital) that persist over time and impact positively on health. Putnam et al. (1993: 167) define social capital as the 'features of social organization such as trust, norms and networks that can improve the efficiency of society by facilitating coordinated actions' and suggest that communities with high and long-established levels of social capital are significantly more successful that those that lack them. We have evidence from school improvement and effectiveness research to confirm that high levels of trust between head teacher and staff, between staff and pupils, and between home and school, are associated with beneficial outcomes (Mortimore and Whitty 1997). This evidence suggests that interventions are needed that shift opportunities towards disadvantaged individuals, families and communities and build social capital. Child-to-Child offers a strategy for building social capital through making schools healthier.

The health transition has important implications for education as a basis for developing a society in which each citizen is equally able to access health information and take health action. Traditional health education curricula in many countries are hopelessly inadequate in equipping students to understand and influence the cultural, social and behavioural determinants of health. Innovative approaches are needed to enable professionals to learn how to work in partnership with individuals and communities. Recognition of this need is behind the recent upsurge of interest in Participatory Rural Appraisal[1] (PRA) approaches, which emphasize learning with and from local people in a relaxed and flexible way using powerful visualization of situations and knowledge generated through dialogue. Recently the abbreviation PLA (Participatory Learning and Action) has been adopted as a collective term to describe the growing body of participatory approaches and methodologies (IIED 1995). As we shall see in Chapter 4, Child-to-Child claims to have kept abreast of current thinking and its methodology is informed by innovative and participatory approaches.

Maternal schooling and health In developing countries there is a strong and well-established link between maternal education and the mortality rates of infants and young children. Evidence for this has been extensively reviewed (Cochrane et al. 1982; Morley and Lovel 1986; Caldwell 1993; World Bank 1993; UNDP 1997). Caldwell (1993) reports the findings of a United Nations study of 15 developing countries, which concluded that child mortality was reduced by 6.8 per cent for each year of maternal education. A study by Hobcraft (1993) comparing data on maternal education and child health from Indonesia, Kenya, Morocco and Peru suggests that where mothers have four or more years of schooling the risk of their children dying before they are two years old is greatly decreased. The World Bank (1993) also reports that well-educated mothers can often manage to reduce the damage that poverty does to health. In the Côte d'Ivoire a survey of rural households showed that 24 per cent of children with uneducated mothers had stunted growth compared to only 11 per cent with mothers who had some schooling. There have also been calls for greater recognition of the impact of a father's education: 'the extraordinary impact of maternal education has tended to obscure the fact that fathers' education, even when controlled for income, also strongly influences child survival in some countries equaling, or even exceeding the influence of mothers' education' (Caldwell 1993).

The important questions are how and why education achieves this impact. The education of fathers appears to work mostly through increasing family income, whereas educating women strengthens their ability to create healthy households and improves their patterns of child care (World Bank 1993). Caldwell (1993) reports on a study in India that identified three factors critical to understanding the impact of maternal education on child health. First, educated mothers assumed that it was only natural for them to take their sick child to the doctor. Second, they spent longer discussing the child's sickness with the doctor. Third, illiterate mothers failed to report lack of success of prescribed treatment because they lacked confidence in confronting a more powerful figure. It would therefore appear that maternal education improves child health by increasing motivation to take better care of children and to begin to develop positive attitudes to, for example, clean water, sanitation, good nutrition and using Western-style health services. Education also increases women's incomes and most importantly their autonomy to act within the family and community.

The literature we have reviewed above provides us with evidence to support investment in education, especially of women and girls, as a means of improving health. This evidence is important because it supports the assumption underlying Child-to-Child that educating children about health can improve their health and that of their families. It is also important because many Child-to-Child programmes (such as the Little Teacher Programme in Botswana) are especially successful at recruiting girls.

Education and HIV/AIDS   The AIDS pandemic presents a strong challenge to education at both macro and micro levels. Not only are the education sectors of many countries faced with the loss of a substantial proportion of their professional workforce but AIDS also has implications for demographic trends, economic productivity and growth, agriculture, social cohesiveness, political stability and ultimately for human resource development (Lewin 1993; Carr-Hill 1994b; Phillips and Verhasselt 1994; Shaeffer 1994). Reduced immunity caused by HIV has also lead to the resurgence of infections such as tuberculosis, which was previously receding in many parts of Africa and Asia. In the absence of any cure, we have only education as a means of preventing further spread of HIV and enabling society to avoid discriminating against, and to care for, those already infected.

AIDS education frequently focuses on individual learning about how to practise 'safer sex'. However, there is a strong argument for broadening the focus to increase understanding of the economic, social, cultural, societal and political motivations that encourage or restrict safer sexual behaviour. The HIV pandemic flourishes where individual capacity to learn and respond has been constrained, generally by belonging to a marginalized or stigmatized group. In many countries, for example, discrimination creates an environment of increased risk for women, linked directly with their unequal role, rights, status and economic position. We can therefore argue that a human rights framework should be used for developing educational programmes to combat AIDS. The school is an important forum for education about HIV and AIDS but this should be developed within a broad-based, comprehensive framework of positive health and well-being. Children need information but equally importantly they need to develop essential life skills such as tolerance, compassion and decision-making powers. The step-by-step educational process advocated by Child-to-Child and given in Chapter 1 is appropriate for developing broad-based sexual health programmes that include a focus on HIV and AIDS.

Health and educational achievement We have a small but rapidly growing body of evidence to link the health and especially the nutritional status of children with their educational achievement. We now know enough to be able to recommend health and nutrition programmes among efforts to increase school enrolment, to decrease absenteeism, repetition and early drop-out rates and to improve classroom performance (Pollitt 1984, 1990; UN ACC/SCN 1990; Ivanovic 1991; World Bank 1993; Levinger 1994). Consequently support for spending on health to increase returns on educational investment is being strongly endorsed by international development agencies:

Educating children at school on health should be given the highest priority, not for their health *per se*, but also from the perspective of education, since if they are to learn they need to be in good health. (Hiroshi Nakajima, director-general of the World Health Organization, WHO 1992: preface)

Children do not come to school as blank slates. Much of their capacity for active leaning is already formed. The effects of school inputs such as teacher training and textbooks depend ultimately on children's capacity to learn from them. The work of Ernesto Pollitt (1990) was instrumental in getting health onto the agenda of the 1990 World Conference on Education and in raising awareness that the remarkable increase in access to education seen in recent years has not been matched by a comparable improvement in the health of the school age population. Pollitt reviews evidence to link health and educability and strongly challenges education planners to take more account of the influence of nutritional status on learning achievement:

> Educational policy-makers and planners have overlooked nutrition and health as determinants of school entry, wastage and attainment. ... poor nutrition and health during the pre-school years can have long-term consequences affecting a child's later progress during the school period. (1990: 13)

Evidence to link nutritional status with educability is also reviewed in the 1993 World Bank Development report, which recommends increased intervention through nutrition education, micronutrient fortification of food, micronutrient supplementation and food price subsidies. Many of these recommendations are directed towards improving the health of the school-age child, and there is currently much interest in the school as an intervention site. A study in Guatemala (Martorell 1992) demonstrated that improved nutrition during early childhood was related to improved intellectual performance in adolescence and adulthood. This suggests that improved nutrition during early childhood has a longer-term pay-off than previously documented.

The nature of the link between nutritional status and educability is complex. It involves problems arising from under-nutrition as well as from specific nutritional deficiencies. Protein energy malnutrition progressively impairs children's intellectual development. A poor diet, intestinal worms and malaria cause iron deficiency anaemia, which is a major cause of irreversible impairment of cognitive ability in pre-school and early school-age children and is also highly prevalent among post-pubertal girls and women. Iodine deficiency, the leading preventable cause of intellectual impairment in the world, causes mental retardation, delayed motor development, stunting of growth, and neuromuscular, speech and hearing disorders. Vitamin A deficiency is the major cause of reduced vision and blindness in children and is linked to increased mortality from infection, especially measles, diarrhoeal diseases and acute respiratory tract infections.

Improving the health of schoolchildren provides a good opportunity for education and health professionals to work closely together. However, differences of approach can be seen among major initiatives in this field. For example, the Partnership for Child Development (Bundy and Hall 1992; WHO 1993) is largely concerned with the implementation and evaluation of a package of medical inputs in schools in five or six countries. These inputs include iron and iodine dietary supplements and de-worming tablets. Health education is included but has not been a priority. In contrast WHO's (1992a) Comprehensive School Health initiative has an increased focus on education for health, as shown below.

Comprehensive school health education Teaching that enables children to survive in their own environment (e.g. what to eat, what to wear, how to keep safe and to observe elementary rules of hygiene) has traditionally been regarded as the function of the home. However, following the World Conference on Education for All (WCEFA 1990) the primary school in most societies is now recognized to be the most efficient way of reaching the child population and consequently there is wider acceptance of the principle that along with the teaching of 'the three Rs' (reading, writing and arithmetic) basic education should provide relevant and appropriate teaching necessary for the survival and health of the individual.

WHO's Comprehensive School Health Initiative is a broad-based inter-sectoral approach, which builds on experience worldwide. It aims to provide the impetus for mobilizing and strengthening health promotion and education activities at the local, national, regional and global levels to improve health through schools. The WHO (1992a) framework for the development of comprehensive school health programmes includes three main components: (i) a comprehensive health service for students and staff; (ii) a healthy school environment; and (iii) comprehensive school health education. Priority is given to the health education component, which is based on a holistic understanding of health, utilizes all educational opportunities for health, and strives to harmonize the health messages and to empower children and youth to take action to improve health.

In November 1994 an updated rationale for the WHO initiative was developed as a background paper for an expert committee meeting on school health. This committee was convened in September 1995. This updated rationale reflects changing priorities within health education and development. In addition to the original three components it includes four more: ensuring optimal use of scarce health and education resources; a positive approach to health promotion; outreach to parents and community; and a move towards equity by raising the standard of schooling and the status of girls and women in the community.

Health and Development

There is a considerable body of literature on health and development, much of which is concerned with a critical debate around the political economy of health (Werner 1977; Doyal 1979; Chambers 1983; Navarro 1984; Sanders 1985; Morley and Lovel 1986). This debate provides a searching analysis of the issues of power and domination both between and within countries in the context of health and development. It has constituted a powerful lobby for change and is further examined below. A useful way into this debate is through Doyal's (1979) sensitive analysis, which addresses concerns around medical practice and the reproduction of labour power under capitalism, the social production of health and illness, and the social production of medical care. There is also a large literature centring on the impact of development policies on health and the impact of health on development policies. (This literature is extensively reviewed by

Weil et al. 1990.) A major underlying theme throughout this literature is that there is no simple one-way correlation between fast development and better health. It is increasingly clear that development is often equated with different health and not simply better health.

A valuable overview of the interrelationships between health and development is provided by Phillips and Verhasselt (1994), who focus on four main issues: (i) the impact of health on global environmental change and on economic adjustment policies; (ii) the potential for incorporating traditional medicine within modern health systems; (iii) cultural and developmental factors underlying the global pattern of HIV/AIDS transmission; and (iv) the impact of the global pharmaceutical industry on health development. This review then considers the impact of these issues on vulnerable groups (women, mothers and children, the elderly), community participation in Primary Health Care and the health of people living in cities in developing countries. Finally, the analysis turns to the realities in specific countries and areas.

During the 1990s two policy issues have dominated the field – the financing of PHC and health systems reforms involving decentralization and participation (World Bank 1993). The tension here is between efficiency and equity, and the question is whether efficiency has overrun equity. This tension is reflected in the way in which the World Bank's 1993 *World Development Report: Investing in Health* has been received in different quarters. The medical establishment in many countries has warmly received the Report as a valuable contribution towards a cost-effective health care strategy, while political activists such as Werner and Saunders (1997: 107) view it as 'a rehash of the conservative strategies that have systematically derailed Comprehensive Primary Health Care ... a disturbing document with dangerous implications'. LaFond (1995: 94) argues that the internal pressures of development institutions cause donors and governments to dictate terms of investment in favour of immediate gains, which frustrates long-term capacity-building and undermines sustainability. She concludes that the central challenge facing investment in health in the 1990s is for governments and donors to develop long-term partnerships to support the gradual strengthening of local capacity to raise, prioritize and manage resources in line with local needs.

There is much parallel thinking reflected in the literatures concerned with theories of health and development and education and development. Consequently a similar framework to that used earlier in this chapter to analyse theories of education and development can also be applied to theories of health and development.

Health for increased productivity and improved returns on education In the period following the Second World War standards of health declined, and investing in health was seen as a means of ensuring both the quantity and productivity of the human capital needed for a productive labour force. Poor health and nutrition were considered undesirable because they reduced labour productivity and impaired the ability to learn, which resulted in a poor return on investments in education and training. The health of mothers was acknowledged to be critical to the health and well-being of children, and was promoted to improve their eventual labour contribution. Similarly, the prevention and control of communicable diseases was pursued because of the heavy toll placed on the economies of less developed countries through treatment costs and lowered productivity.

The response of WHO to post-war decline in standards of health was oriented towards disease control. During the 1950s WHO favoured mass vertical campaigns to control diseases such as malaria, tuberculosis and trachoma. These campaigns delivered a simple technological 'fix' such as DDT spraying or the administration of dapone. During the 1960s WHO began to integrate these major programmes with general health services and to emphasize what they called Basic Health Services. In 1967 the emphasis shifted again to promoting health planning. In line with the thinking encapsulated in modernization theory, importance was given to the acceptance of modern values, attitudes and behaviour, informed by biomedical science, as the basis for health development. Consequently traditional healers and their practices were seen as old-fashioned and were derided.

The political economy of health During the 1970s, in the face of growing inequities between rich and poor both between and within countries, disillusionment with existing systems of health care set in. As we saw earlier in this chapter the economic model of education and development had become the subject of acrimonious debate centring on education as production or reproduction. This debate fuelled a parallel debate around the political economy of health. Those who favoured Marxist and neo-Marxist perspectives argued for radical change within health systems in capitalist-oriented society. They saw the existing model of medical care as a highly significant factor in the reproduction of both the forces and relations of production. Consequently they argued that healthy children would themselves grow up to be the parents of healthy children because they had the means to access health (and education services) and because the system was self-reproducing. We saw in Chapter 2 that Illich followed his thesis on 'deschooling society' (Illich 1973) with a parallel attack on the power of the medical profession in his much quoted essay 'The epidemics of modern medicine' (Illich 1976). With this thesis he helped to prepare the way for the reorientation of health services towards Primary Health Care. An equally savage attack was made by Doyal (1979) on capitalist and neo-capitalist expansion in the Third World, which she claimed had systematically undermined the health of the population and created obstacles to the realization of effective health policies in these countries.

The search for new paths to learning and to health care intensified throughout the 1970s and resulted in the two milestones in development thinking, the Faure Report (Faure et al. 1972) and the Alma Ata Declaration (WHO 1978), which have been discussed earlier in this chapter. These documents advocated reform of health education systems towards greater equity and strongly influenced the original formulation of Child-to-Child. Traditional medicine and those who practised it were now welcomed as partners for health, and a new cadre of health worker was defined. This was the community health worker, who was to be the agent of change to enable the community to become empowered and to fully participate in health development. When the paradigm shift in development thinking occurred at the end of the 1980s health was acknowledged to be an integral part of development, social productivity was intimately related to economic productivity and in 1990 indicators of health and nutritional status were included for the first time as measures of development (UNDP 1990).

The impact on health of debt and structural adjustment Health expenditure has been falling in many countries. Stewart (1991) presents evidence to demonstrate that social sector spending per capita declined by 26 per cent in Africa and 18 per cent in Latin America between 1980 and 1985. A common proposition advanced to explain this reduction is that health has been 'crowded out' by escalating debt. It is plausible that high levels of debt servicing are related to lower levels of social sector expenditure. Today, many countries owe more in debt principle and interest than they earn from exports (Gardner 1995). Concern for the impact of national debt on children has prompted UNICEF (1991) to voice a strong warning:

> children are still paying heavily for their nation's debts; and the currency they are paying with is their opportunity for normal growth, their opportunity to be educated, and often their *lives*. ... it is the antithesis of civilization that so many millions of children should be continuing to pay such a price. (1991: 11)

Structural adjustment programmes have also contributed to reduced social sector spending and been linked to lowered health status (Werner and Saunders 1997). Education, arguably more important to long-term health than the provision of curative medical services, has also suffered from these austerity programmes. Programmes of economic adjustment, developed in line with World Bank policy and imposed on countries as a loan condition, have been particularly criticized for failing to show adequate concern for the impact of their policies on the poor and most vulnerable groups in society, especially women and children. In many countries stabilization and adjustment policies in combination with other factors have been shown to have an adverse impact on the poorest (Lewin 1993). This adverse impact has led to calls for compensatory programmes to protect the basic health and nutrition of low-income groups and for the monitoring of living standards, health and nutrition (Cornia et al. 1987). UNICEF (1991) stress that social 'safety nets' should be a prime responsibility of the state to alleviate the detrimental effects of structural adjustment programmes on the health of the poor.

The World Bank has published programme evaluations from Sri Lanka, Brazil and Chile demonstrating that not only can the poor be protected but their living standards and health status can improve during structural adjustment (Measham 1986). Despite such success stories the World Bank continues to attract criticism for its role in the promotion of such policies. Phillips and Verhasselt (1994: 305) contend that attempts made to recoup expenditure through the so-called 'cost recovery' schemes (especially in Africa since the. 1987 Bamako Initiative) will further exclude the poorest and most needy from access to essential drugs. The NGO community has continued to argue strongly that structural adjustment policies are widening the gap between rich and poor. In 1994 a relatively small NGO in the UK called Christian Aid launched a brave campaign under the slogan 'Who rules the World?' which publicly challenged the World Bank to enter into dialogue over the effects of its structural adjustment policy on the poor.

The movement of populations During the 1990s there has been unprecedented movement of populations in response to war, conflict and political violence, and natural disasters such as floods, hurricanes and earthquakes. In many areas of Africa, South-East Asia, the former Soviet Union and former Yugoslavia there are now huge numbers of displaced persons and refugees who have special health and educational needs. They need shelter and without adequate food they become malnourished. They are often physically and psychologically traumatized. Moreover, huge numbers of displaced persons place intolerable burdens on the resources of poor host countries. Population movements are widely recognized to be an important cause of disease diffusion and have been implicated in the spread of cholera, malaria and HIV infection.

Conflict also disrupts health, education and welfare services and such disruption can be seriously damaging in the long term. In areas of conflict it is difficult to sustain preventive services such as immunization and to sustain disease eradication programmes. Community conflict inevitably results in the breakdown of programmes dependent on local participation. The need for curative and rehabilitative services increases and the diversion of economic resources and human energies into violence and struggle for survival means there is less available for health, education and welfare. Child-to-Child has recognized the special needs of children living under especially difficult circumstances and has developed health learning materials to help children living in refugee camps (Hanbury 1993).

Environmental change and health   Damage to the environment may harm human health and economic productivity and it is currently receiving a high profile on international agendas and in the media. The 1992 *World Development Report* of the World Bank has a particular focus on development and the environment and the WHO (1992b) report *Our Planet Our Earth* provides a comprehensive overview of the major issues. The *World Development Report* (World Bank 1992: 4) identifies priority health hazards caused by environmental mis-management (water pollution, water scarcity, air pollution, solid and hazardous wastes, soil degradation, deforestation, loss of biodiversity and atmospheric changes) and identifies the consequences of these health hazards for productivity. The report argues that environmental degradation is increasing but that its extent varies between countries and with the nature and stage of industrialization. Consequently it recommends that each country needs to assess the extent of its own environmental degradation and set its own priorities.

Health and development policies   There are many documented cases of adverse health effects resulting from physical development schemes (Borini 1986; Weil et al. 1990; Phillips and Verhasselt 1994). Dams, hydroelectric schemes and irrigation projects have often increased the incidence of water-related diseases such as malaria, bilharzia and hookworm (Hunter et al. 1993). Increasing industrialization in many countries brings increased risks to health where legislation, environ-mental and health-and-safety controls are not yet in place. Many workers, including children, in industry, agriculture and other sectors are at daily risk from exposure to occupational health hazards, toxic substances and exploitative workplace practices. Economic develop-ment has been adversely affected where access to fertile areas and valuable natural resources have been restricted by the presence of disease vectors. In order to develop such areas many large programmes have been supported by the World Bank to eradicate diseases such as onchocerciasis (river blindness) in West Africa, trypanosomiasis (sleeping sickness) in Nigeria and malaria in Brazil and Indonesia (Measham 1986).

In this chapter we have reviewed the literature on education and health in the context of development to help us understand the context in which Child-to-Child was originally formulated and to assess its claim to have continued to keep abreast of current thinking. The literature reviewed has also provided considerable evidence to support the assumptions underlying Child-to-Child, which are that education can improve health and that healthy children learn better at school.

Note

1. PRA is a 'systematic research methodology that actively involves community members in identifying, analysing and solving their problems' (UNICEF 1996).

II

A Critical Analysis of the Child-to-Child Approach

4

Child-to-Child: the Parameters

In this chapter we look more critically at Child-to-Child. We examine the theories and concepts underlying the original formulation of the approach and see how Child-to-Child has responded to innovation and change. We consider how far ideas developed largely in the West can be used in contexts where the role and status of children in society are viewed differently. This chapter draws on primary and secondary analyses of the literature on Child-to-Child and on interview data.[1]

Overview of the Origins and Early Dissemination of Child-to-Child

We saw in Chapter 2 that new paths to learning and to health care were being actively sought during the 1970s (Freire 1972; Faure et al. 1972; Coombs 1968; Dore 1976; WHO 1978). Social responsibility, altruism and the fostering of pupils helping each other to learn was regarded as 'wholly desirable' (Foot et al. 1990: 3) and helped to set the climate for Child-to-Child. The General Assembly of the United Nations officially designated 1979 the International Year of the Child and challenged all countries to critically review the programmes provided for children and consider how children's rights could be safeguarded and their lives bettered.

This challenge was the catalyst for the development of Child-to-Child. Otto Wolff, then professor of child health at London University's Institute of Child Health, recalled that in 1977 he was approached to develop an initiative within the framework of the UN Year of the Child and a small grant was made available by what was then the British Ministry of Overseas Development. Wolff invited a colleague at the Institute of Child Health, Dr David Morley, who was working in what was then the Tropical Child Health Unit, to undertake this task. Morley had a considerable international reputation for innovative thinking and was an opinion leader in the Primary Health Care movement. Guthrie (1991) recalled that:

> Morley's original idea was based on what he had seen all over the less developed world, namely that older children in a family spend much of their time looking after their younger siblings. This existing relationship could, he believed, be used and developed for the informal teaching of health matters to the younger children in a community.

At an early stage Morley's ideas were shared with colleagues in what was then the Department of Education in Developing Countries at the university's sister Institute of Education. One of these colleagues, Hugh Hawes, played a central role in developing and disseminating the ideas and became the first director of the Child-to-Child Trust in 1988. Another member of what Guthrie called the 'inner circle' was Beverly Young, an educationist with the British Council who remained actively involved until his untimely death in 1991. Two other members of this group were David Werner and Stephen Varistandsel. Guthrie recalled the enormous drive and great excitement among this group of 'enthusiastic evangelists' who shared strong bonds of personal friendship as well as a firm commitment to building sustainable partnerships for child health and education. How far the success of Child-to-Child has continued to rely on the crusading spirit of its founding fathers (and how far it can succeed without their inspiration) will be discussed later.

It was agreed that an educational approach would be developed and two meetings were convened in April 1977 to undertake the task. Twenty people from 13 countries formed the first working party in London. At a subsequent working party in Fittleworth in Sussex they were joined by 22 others from 13 further countries. The Fittleworth meeting was chaired by Tom Lambo, then deputy director of WHO, whose involvement reflected the interest shown by international agencies from the start. This meeting brought together experienced practitioners and renowned academics with the intention that dreams would be tailored to the realities of life.

The preface to the report of these meetings (CHILD-to-child 1978) provides a clear statement of the original conceptualization of Child-to-Child: 'An international programme designed to teach and encourage school children to concern themselves with the health, welfare and development of their younger brothers and sisters and of other young children in the community.' The programme was unusual in that from the outset it was formulated not as a single blueprint to be applied to every situation but as a reservoir of ideas to be taken and adapted for use as starting points for developing more ideas.

The focus of the programme was to be the needs of children in rural and urban areas of poor countries. The needs of poor children in developed countries were deliberately excluded and consequently many people still regard Child-to-Child as solely a programme for children in developing countries. With hindsight it may be asked whether the potential applicability of Child-to-Child ideas to the developed world should not have been affirmed from the outset. The general principles were defined as 'respect and concern for children; belief that older children have a role to play in promoting the health of their younger brothers and sisters; understanding that there are ways in which this may be achieved' (CHILD-to-child 1978: 45). The activities were grouped under five headings: 'eating well, children as health workers, providing a healthy environment, children growing up and stimulating younger children' (ibid.: 25). At this early stage there was little recognition of the special needs of disabled children and those living in especially difficult circumstances. However, there was recognition of the delicate balance that exists between encouraging and building on children's developing altruism, and exploiting their use as parent substitutes without providing the support that children need (ibid.: 2). In practice this delicate balance has not always been achieved.

From the start it was also realized that parents might be influenced by the health messages brought home from school, but according to Guthrie (1991) it was understood that this would not be the main thrust of the programme. Upper-case letters were chosen for the first 'CHILD' to represent 'the big child' and lower-case for the second 'child' to represent 'the small child'. Guthrie (1991) felt that this mixing of upper- and lower-case letters was useful 'as a gimmick to help the programme catch on and to visually reflect the idea of the big child looking after the small child'. This gimmick undoubtedly appealed to some people and it is still used today by organizations such as the CHILD-to-child Network of Botswana. However, as the concept has evolved the original mix of upper- and lower-case letters has become increasingly inappropriate, and Child-to-Child being written in different ways has in some areas caused confusion.

Early dissemination of the ideas The original formulation of the concept was disseminated in the first book, *CHILD-to-child* (Aarons et al. 1979). It contained health education materials called Activity Sheets, developed during the preliminary meetings. This book was regarded by Guthrie as the movement's 'bible'. It was copyright-free but provided little guidance on how the ideas might be used. Children were promoted as health workers and teachers working alongside adults as contributors, as well as receivers of Child-to-Child ideas. The emphasis was on the contribution that schools could make. The contribution of other community groups was not sufficiently acknowledged. The ideas were taken up most rapidly by community groups who were most able to adapt them to the local context. Recognition of the dangers as well as the benefits of promoting children as change agents in traditional societies is reflected in the sentence: '*No children should ever be placed in a position where they appear to be criticising or contradicting their parents or elders*' (Aarons et al. 1979: 14) – the only one of the book's recommendations to be printed in italics for greater emphasis. The opening passage and accompanying illustrations reflect the innovative 'style' of the approach (Figure 4.1).

In the first two years the Child-to-Child co-ordination unit in London, administered by Guthrie, operated from a small office in the Institute of Child Health. This unit defined its aims as:

- to generate and publish ideas and materials related to the role children could play in helping others to improve their health
- to assist in the discussion and clarification of ways in which such ideas and materials could be effectively disseminated and their effect monitored

We know someone who is a teacher and a health worker. She looks after two children. One is four and one is two. She keep them safe. She carries the little one and picks him up when he cries. She protects the bigger one from accidents. Yesterday when the little girl went too near the stove she scolded her. Today she helped her to cross the road and taught her how to watch for the cars. Who is this teacher who does so much for her pupils and does it so well? She is their elder sister – and she is eleven years old …

We know a group of community workers who know every inch of the village in which they work, who are accepted by everyone, who want to help their community, who will work hard (for short periods of time) and cheerfully (all the time). Last month the health worker used them to collect information about which children had been vaccinated in the village. Next Tuesday some of them will help to remind the villagers that the baby clinic is coming and they will be at hand to play with the older children when mothers take their babies to see the nurse. Next month they plan to help the school-teacher in a village clean-up campaign. These health workers are the boys and girls of the village.

Figure 4.1 CHILD-to-child: teachers and health workers
(*source*: adapted from Aarons et al. 1979: 6).

- to facilitate the exchange of information between sectors, agencies and countries concerning the ideas, their dissemination and their effect. (Somerset 1987: vi)

Two years later Guthrie commissioned Marie-Thérèse Feuerstein to produce the first evaluation of Child-to-Child. She analysed information received from 113 respondents in at least 57 countries. Programmes had been introduced by individuals from the fields of health, education and community development, nearly 40 per cent of whom worked on a voluntary basis. At least one and a quarter million children were involved worldwide, more than half of whom were in formal education, but nearly 20 per cent had never been to school. Feuerstein noted that a gap had already opened between theory and practice. The original principle of 'belief that older children have a role to play in promoting the health of their younger brothers and sisters' was reflected in practice, but the other principles had been disregarded. Concern for children themselves, always fundamental to the philosophy of Child-to-Child, was not always evident in practice. This is not entirely surprising considering the low position frequently occupied by children in the social hierarchy and the way in which traditional patterns of child rearing centre on teaching children to respect and even to fear their elders. Feuerstein also found that many programmes lacked understanding of the child-centred educational process promoted by Child-to-Child, which aims to challenge children to think and to solve problems. Before anything else the Child-to-Child approach requires a change of mind on the part of those adopting it.

Growth and development during the 1980s and 1990s As Child-to-Child continued to be spread rapidly, a steering committee was formed to judge how best to respond to requests for assistance, but no attempt was made to oversee development and influence the way in which Child-to-Child ideas were interpreted in practice. In response to deepening understanding of the power of the ideas and experience of the different ways in which it was being implemented, the initial focus on better sibling care broadened. Figure 4.2 shows that it now included the power of children to influence their own age group, their families and community. These developments were acknowledged by a change in capitalization from CHILD-to-child to Child-to-Child. This was a most appropriate change and was welcomed by Dr Pam Zinkin, a colleague at the Institute of Child Health, because it allowed for the fact that disabled children might be older than those who were helping them. However, Guthrie regretted this change, believing that the original 'idiosyncratic mix of letters' helped Child-to-Child ideas to catch on quickly.

During the 1980s the Child-to-Child Trust sought to move away from the earlier notion that Child-to-Child ideas constituted a health education programme. Hawes stated that Child-to-Child 'prefers to see itself as an approach or movement' (1988: 25). This shift was an attempt to discourage people from thinking of Child-to-Child as a single blueprint and from supposing that they now had the panacea

Care for younger children

Care for children of their own age

Influence family members

Spread health ideas and messages in the community

Figure 4.2 The broader conceptualization of Child-to-Child (*source*: Morley and Pridmore 1993).

for all health education problems. The further aim was to encourage and facilitate the use of Child-to-Child ideas and methods within existing programmes not owned by the Child-to-Child Trust. Those who shaped the thinking of Child-to-Child saw that there can be no copyright on good ideas, and welcomed the possibility that the Child-to-Child approach should be taken up and applied as widely as possible.

It is doubtful whether the attempts to make clearer what Child-to-Child is and what it is not have succeeded. Child-to-Child is still commonly viewed as a programme in which children teach other children about health. Furthermore, where Child-to-Child ideas have been taken up by others what is then made of them cannot easily be monitored or assessed. Relinquishing control of the ideas has risked forfeiting the possibility of evaluating their effectiveness.

During the late 1980s (in the run-up to the 1991 World Conference on Education for All) greater emphasis was given to the educational nature of Child-to-Child and to the approach being used within the formal education system – where the largest mass of children could be reached – and within teacher education. The concept of 'child power' was extended beyond the framework of Primary Health Care and into educational and environmental development. Children were increasingly valued as a rich resource for community development. The original focus of Child-to-Child on children aged between seven and ten was extended to acknowledge that effective approaches to active learning and social development need to be a continuous process extending from home through pre-school to primary school and beyond. Carnegie and Hawes contend that continuity of approach is paramount: 'Once the chain is broken and the child perceives that he is no longer invited to find out, ask questions, solve problems and co-operate with others then serious damage is done to the child and ultimately to the community in which that child lives' (1990: 50).

During the 1990s the Trust has identified three main foci for its work: (i) promoting health through schooling; (ii) working with children in especially difficult circumstances (refugee children living in camps, children who live and work on the street and children affected by war and conflict); and (iii) encouraging the development of local resource units.

Child-to-Child Ideas and Methodology

To understand more fully what Child-to-Child now claims to have become it is important to examine the components shown in Figure 4.3. The extent to which Child-to-Child is a model of health education and community development needs to be critically considered, as does the claim that Child-to-Child is at once a model of a development agency and a worldwide network concerned with implementation and advocacy.

Child-to-Child acknowledges that children should never be put in a position where they are openly confronting the attitudes and values of their elders, but aims to empower them as communicators of innovation in health and nutrition to families and communities. The Child-to-Child methodology (described in Chapter 1) promotes traditional

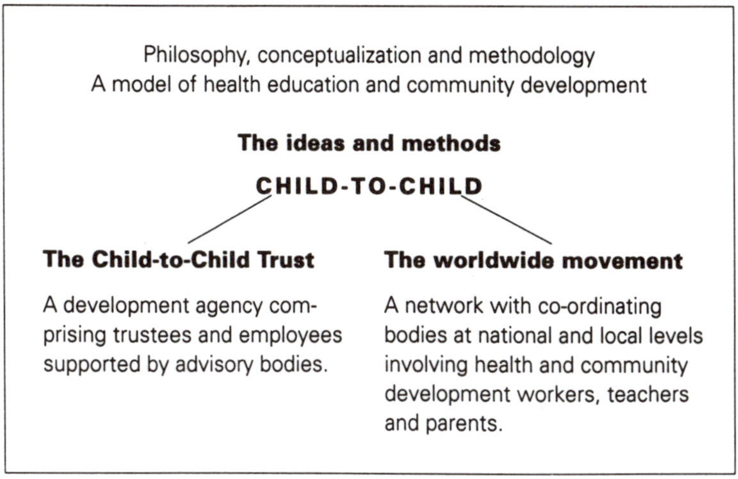

Philosophy, conceptualization and methodology
A model of health education and community development

The ideas and methods

CHILD-TO-CHILD

The Child-to-Child Trust

A development agency comprising trustees and employees supported by advisory bodies.

The worldwide movement

A network with co-ordinating bodies at national and local levels involving health and community development workers, teachers and parents.

Figure 4.3 An overview of Child-to-Child

pedagogy in using song and dance but rejects traditional didactic teaching. This tension between respect for tradition and commitment for change within the conceptualization of Child-to-Child is a sophisticated approach more easily understood – at least by those trained to handle ideas – than applied in the field, where the risk will always be that traditional assumptions about the role of the child will prevail.

As we saw in Chapter 1, the underlying philosophy of Child-to-Child continues to derive from a deep commitment to Primary Health Care, children as agents, and partnerships for health. It reflects faith in the power of children to spread health messages and health practices together with the conviction that they should enjoy and profit from doing so. The use of terms such as 'commitment', 'faith' and 'conviction' reflects the strongly held beliefs of the advocates of Child-to-Child in the truth and importance of their cause. Such a belief, however, is not shared by most of the communities where Child-to-Child ideas are being implemented, societies where adults hold a very different view of children – a view strongly held but unexamined and rarely articulated. Resistance to the principle of children as agents of change by those whose assumptions about children are very different from those of Western and Westernized societies will prove as formidable an obstacle to the implementation of Child-to-Child as the structural, economic and social conditions that impede its realization in practice. It is more difficult to change minds than to sink wells, but it may be more worthwhile.

The Child-to-Child methodology has been reflected in the core learning materials called Activity Sheets, which are published by the Trust in London. These Activity Sheets have continued to focus on priority health issues, provide up-to-date health information and suggest activities intended to be both achievable and enjoyable for children (as we shall further examine in Chapter 5). Since 1978 the original reservoir of ideas has been continually expanded, revised and updated. The Child-to-Child *Resource Book Part One* (1994a) published 40 Activity Sheets grouped into 8 categories. Recently added categories reflect current health concerns identified in Chapter 3: 'Recognizing and helping the disabled', 'Safe life styles' and 'Children living in difficult circumstances'. Experience has shown that these Activity Sheets do little good unless adapted to the local situation and incorporated into carefully structured lesson plans. This must be done without what is distinctively 'Child-to-Child' about the material being lost. It is at this point, where the material is being modified for local use, that there is the danger that it is transposed into something else, more congenial to those used to more didactic styles of education.

This is important work because there is an urgent need to develop classroom health learning materials that most teachers can use. Existing materials that incorporate the Child-to-Child methodology rely both on the willingness of teachers to alter the traditional relationship between themselves and their pupils and on their skills in active learning methods and classroom management. Many teachers have neither the willingness nor the skills. It is therefore important to find out what teaching methods most teachers are using in the classroom and to develop lesson guides that build on these methods. Guides should introduce at least one activity requiring children to find out something outside the classroom – at home or in the community. Such guides need to be developed and tried out locally before being finalized and published in a particular country.

The rapid spread of ideas As we saw in Chapter 1, Child-to-Child ideas have spread rapidly around the world. We would argue that Child-to-Child's progress can largely be attributed to the personalities and drive of the founding members (especially Morley, Guthrie, Wolff, Hawes, Werner, Young and Vanistandsel) together with the force and appeal of its ideas (Carnegie 1991). Perhaps more significant as an explanation of its international growth has been the extent to which Child-to-Child has appealed to and has been endorsed at the highest professional and political levels – although this positive response is itself testimony to the eloquent advocacy of the powerful individuals who were lobbying for Child-to-Child at these levels. Morley (1993) acknowledges the extent to which the spread of Child-to-Child has been secured by continuing support from the British Council, the Aga Khan Foundation, and UNICEF country offices. In 1991 UNICEF publicly endorsed the work of the Child-to-Child Trust, presenting it with the Maurice Pate Award. In his presentation speech James Grant (then director-general of UNICEF) stated that the award was given in recognition of Child-to-Child's 'extraordinary and exemplary leadership in and contribution to the survival, protection and development of children worldwide'.

Many cultures, especially in Africa and Asia, have a powerful tradition of learning from great teachers. For example, in Tanzania former President Julius Nyerere has always been known to his people as *Mwalimu* (teacher). This tradition has facilitated dissemination of Child-to-Child ideas because renowned and charismatic teachers have actively promoted them with the full support of their organizations behind them. Being based at the University of London has enabled the Trust more easily to build up an expert and influential group of teachers and scholars to support and contribute to the cause. Child-to-Child has benefited from the support of the international development agencies and capitalized on publicity and political will for change engendered by major WHO declarations, the World Summit for Children and the World Conference on Education for All.

This style of dissemination is not without its associated problems of dependency and paternalism. It is an irony that a movement that seeks to win its way by the strength of its ideas, and that moreover holds up those who are traditionally least influential in society as potent instruments for change, should owe its growth to such an extent to powerful individuals and prestigious institutions. However, devolving authority from the Trust has meant that important centres like CHETNA, ARC and CISAS could claim Child-to-Child as their own and 'run with it'. This trend towards devolution has continued during the 1990s with further strengthening of these centres and new centres developing in countries such as Ghana.

All these factors have encouraged the rapid uptake of Child-to-Child ideas. It therefore becomes all the more important to recognize the fundamental problems in the dissemination of its methodology. As mentioned above, few adults have yet developed the special under-standing and skills needed to work with children in a truly partici-patory way. There is little recognition that activity on its own is not enough: activity without understanding is not empowering. There is also a tension between the time needed for activities and the pressures of academic success. Stephens (1993: 12) endorses this point. He records that teachers in Uganda are arguing that in order to be accorded more time and higher status, health education should become part of the mainstream assessed curriculum. However, such a development would threaten the child-centred nature of the approach and diminish its potential for health action and community impact.

The Child-to-Child Trust In 1988 Child-to-Child was constituted as a charitable Trust jointly sponsored by the University of London Institutes of Education and Child Health. Its priorities were to keep up to date with emerging health needs and issues and to encourage the spread of Child-to-Child to the North as well as the South (Child-to-Child 1990).

The Trust, though not itself a development agency, provides an interesting model of how such an agency can be organized. The London office has always been small and highly cost-efficient. Until recently it employed a director, a programme officer and an adminis-trative assistant. Following the resignation of the last director the Trust has recently been restructured. The executive secretary now works closely with a small number of designated 'Child-to-Child partners' who have been instrumental in the development of Child-to-Child and give freely of their time and expertise. The Trust continues to rely on the support of volunteers who work in the office as well as a wide group of UK advisers and a smaller group of international advisers who are actively committed to promoting Child-to-Child in their regions and internationally. Those who 'believe in' Child-to-Child promote its ideas with a commitment born of the faith that those ideas are important and true. The surviving members of Guthrie's original 'inner circle' remain prophetic figures and are still widely regarded in developing countries as 'gurus', a role that, whatever their own wishes, they have found difficult to relinquish. Hawes (1991) rejects the notion of the Trust as a development agency, viewing it rather as a model of aid:

> Child-to-Child has been demonstrably and amazingly successful as a pattern of aid. The fact that such an enormous amount of change take-up has been achieved by a tiny little unit working on a shoestring has demonstrated the value of high-class professional involvement. One of the things that Child-to-Child has always stressed is that everything it sends out should be backed by the very highest expertise and sent out in a free flow situation without strings of ownership. This is an extremely important pattern.

Despite such claims, many health and education workers in the developing world still view Child-to-Child as a health education programme. They are often under the misconception that it is a programme developed for the UK and exported to developing countries, and they most commonly consider the Trust as 'just another pot of money' to be tapped for programme development. The critical question is whether the true character of Child-to-Child – a fund of ideas rather than a fund of money – is easily grasped by health workers and others in developing countries conditioned to perceive aid largely in terms of financial and material help.

The Trust has always claimed to see the need to develop a *modus operandi* in line with the ethos of its guiding principles. It has sought to adopt a non-directive organizational culture and style of leadership and to set up structures to stimulate ideas and facilitate sharing of experiences around the world. These structures include correspondence with individuals, the production and dissemination of an annual newsletter and report, and frequent participation in national and regional meetings and workshops. The organizational culture is also reflected in the style of meetings – people are encouraged to share experiences and learn from each other and are given support and encouragement to increase their self-confidence and motivation. Great importance is accorded to developing and maintaining a strong and positive group dynamic, which is relaxed but enthusiastic and acknowledges the unique contribution each participant makes. The importance of a social programme is fully recognized. This approach has helped to build up a committed and capable caucus of advocates for Child-to-Child. Providing financial support and resource persons for such meetings and workshops around the world has proved to be a most effective strategy for dissemination and feedback of Child-to-Child ideas and practice.

In close co-operation with the Child-to-Child Trust a similar organization, L'Enfant pour L'Enfant, was founded in 1984 to reach out to Francophone countries. This organization has an office in the Institute of Health and Development at the University of Paris and also draws on the resources of the Centre for Research in Education and Health in Liège (Belgium), the International Catholic Children's Bureau (ICCB) and a network of African partners. Child-to-Child and L'Enfant pour L'Enfant both promote child-centred approaches to health education and are currently orientated towards primary school-aged children. However, L'Enfant pour L'Enfant is rather more directive in approach.

The worldwide movement that has grown up around Child-to-Child has been described in Chapter 1. Within the movement the Trust plays an important role in helping to strengthen links between regions and countries. It also acts as a clearing-house for information and has published directories of Child-to-Child initiatives to disseminate details of activities and contact persons around the world

Child-to-Child and Global Development Goals

We saw in Chapter 1 that Child-to-Child has been shaped by three milestones in development thinking: the Declarations of Health for All (WHO 1978), the Rights of the Child (UNICEF 1990) and Education for All (WCEFA 1990). These Declarations, made in recognition of growing concern that the world's health and education systems

Figure 4.4 The Child-to-Child conceptualization of health
(*source*: adapted from Hawes and Scotchmer 1993: 14).

are in crisis, have stimulated wide-ranging debate on effective strategies and approaches to achieve their ambitious goals.

Primary Health Care   Within this framework Child-to-Child endorses
the rights and responsibilities of children to participate and recognizes
their enormous potential for improving health. Child-to-Child operates
with a broad model of health that includes physical, mental and social
dimensions and acknowledges the interaction of environmental
factors (see Figure 4.4).

The rights of the child   Child-to-Child ideas and methods are also integral to achieving the goals embedded in the Convention on the Rights of the Child (UNCRC 1989). Alongside the rights to protection and provision, the Convention specifically endorses the rights of a child to participate. A crucial principle of the Convention is that children must be given a voice and their views and opinions respected and acted on. Article 12 states that:

> Parties shall assure to the child who is capable of forming his or her own views the right to express those views freely in all matters affecting the child, the views of the child being given due weight in accordance with the age and maturity of the child. (UNCRC 1989)

The Convention is now the most widely ratified document of international law in the history of human rights, but signing the Convention is one thing and meaningful practice is another. We need to pay attention to the gap between rhetoric and reality and consider the impact of culture on what children are allowed to participate in and whose ends their participation is serving.

At the heart of Child-to-Child is the right of a child to participate as a subject and not merely as an object of development. However, Child-to-Child stresses the need to balance rights with responsibilities: 'Just as adult citizens have rights and duties towards health, so do children' (Hawes and Scotchmer 1993: 16) (see Figure 4.5). Clearly the nature and degree of moral responsibility in childhood is a large and complex issue, but Child-to-Child is surely right in recognizing the growing capacity of children to take responsibility for themselves and others. Partnership with children is important because partners are people whom you respect and work with. Accepting children as partners helps them develop and enhances their feelings of worth not only in their own eyes but also in the eyes of adults.

But the notion of partnership with children is complex and can be problematic. If children's participation as partners is not to be mere tokenism, adults need to be flexible, and willing to trust children and to work alongside them. Working with children as partners requires that adults open their minds to the notion of partnership with children and that they stop to listen to children. The real challenge is for adults to let go of the control traditionally exercised over children and to learn to work with them as partners without imposing participation

Figure 4.5 Children as citizens (*source*: Hawes and Scotchmer 1993).

on them or expecting tireless devotion to task. Adults need to find the right balance between giving too much and too little guidance and to learn when to follow and when to offer practical advice and support. Although children's participation in the work of the family and particularly in child care is traditional, the notion of children as partners in the decision-making processes is both new and radical, and some would argue that it is neither desirable nor achievable. It remains to be seen how far Child-to-Child will ever overcome traditional resistance to admitting children to the decision-making process.

Education for All Within the framework of Education for All (elaborated in Chapter 1) Child-to-Child poses two fundamental questions. First, how can the content of basic education be reformed so that it reflects the real conditions in schools and the real needs of the children who attend them and of the parents who make sacrifices to send them to school? Second, how do we define quality in school health education? To start answering these questions it is useful to compare the innovative ideology of Child-to-Child with the traditional model of health education dominant in the world today. Traditional health education reflects what Freire has termed the 'banking approach' to learning (see Chapter 2). The teacher possesses the medical know-ledge, which he or she passes on to the children, often through rote learning. The aim is to implant healthy and hygienic habits in each child and direct him or her towards a healthy lifestyle. Effectiveness is measured by the extent to which the learner implements the suggested activity. This model is fundamentally flawed because it emphasizes action by the individual rather than by the community. By focusing on 'lifestyle' it ignores 'life context' in which social, cultural and environmental factors are major determinants of health. Consequently this model of health education is ineffective. This point is endorsed by Stephens: '[Traditional health education] has had a negligible influence upon what children actually learn in the classroom, particularly when assessed in terms of community impact' (1993: 4).

Child-to-Child promotes an alternative model of health education, which recognizes the wide range of influences on children's health and attempts to take account of their pre-existing beliefs, values and attitudes. By focusing on the concepts of empowerment and active learning it claims the potential to develop children's capabilities and to enable them to understand their world better. These two concepts lie at the heart of Child-to-Child and are seen as the key to realizing its educational potential. They reflect the fundamental principle that the child should understand. This point is elaborated by Somerset:

> The central and indispensable component of active learning is 'inner activity' in which the learner constructs and reconstructs his system of knowledge, skills and values ... As learning progresses, the ideas system becomes more complex, and in consequence a better model for understanding the outside world and acting in it. (1987: 151)

Quite clearly, health education is much more than conveying health information. It involves a complex and difficult process of learning, relearning and unlearning that presents a strong challenge to traditional pedagogic practice in schools. Many schools are good at conveying facts and many children are good at memorizing them. However, few schools are able to involve all children in the kind of active learning that helps them to understand relevant health issues, encourages them to take responsibility and develops their capabilities for useful health action.

This is where Child-to-Child becomes important as an alternative approach to basic teaching and learning. Many educators recognize Child-to-Child as a means of bringing active learning 'through the back door' into schools that use traditional methods (Phinney and Evans 1992/3). Child-to-Child demands that teachers adopt a new way of working with children that involves them in active learning. The teacher has to become a facilitator, challenging children to think critically about local health issues and helping them to understand these issues at their own developmental level. The teacher has to help them plan, implement and evaluate useful and enjoyable health action based on a realistic assessment of the role which children can play. The question is how far the majority of teachers, particularly in communities where such an approach to children is quite novel, can be expected to develop such skills.

The active learning approach advocated by Child-to-Child does not need to be limited to health education. Evans advocates extending the approach, arguing that the more it is seen as a way to 'help teachers do their job better ... [and] help teachers teach more easily the things they had found difficult, the more readily it is incorporated into a teacher's repertoire of behaviours' (1993: 6). The potential of the methodology for improving the quality of basic education is recognized by the Child-to-Child Trust, which confines its own work within a broad conceptualization of health but actively encourages others to extend the methodology to different fields.

Child-to-Child: Critique and Ways Forward

Child-to-Child is open to a number of criticisms. First, evidence for Child-to-Child's effectiveness is weak. Second, Child-to-Child's approach has not been clearly defined. Third, where Child-to-Child is misunderstood there is the risk of children being exploited. Fourth, Child-to-Child may be failing to recognize the realities of life for schoolchildren in many countries. Fifth, Child-to-Child seriously underestimates the resistance that will be encountered in traditional non-Western cultures to its ideas about children. Finally, as a movement Child-to-Child, despite its claims to the contrary, is still too strongly influenced by the inspiration and influence of its founding fathers.

The need for further evidence for its effectiveness The flexibility and adaptability of Child-to-Child has enabled it to be adopted in a wide range of contexts. Child-to-Child has been used in primary schools (and the communities they serve), in pre-school programmes, in teacher training colleges, with non-formal groups such as Scouts, Guides and youth groups, with refugees and street children, in health training programmes and in health centres. One consequence of this diversity is that there has been little systematic attempt to analyse what can be accomplished by the approach. What evidence there is has been reviewed in Chapter 1.

Heslop (1991) and Lansdown (1995) have argued the need for ethnographically based accounts to illuminate the context into which Child-to-Child is implanted, and for controlled impact studies on health behaviours or status using rigorous design. These research needs are also recognized by the Child-to-Child research group in London. However, Hawes (1991) has questioned the weight placed upon quantitative impact measurements and has called for more studies to evaluate the effects on the child of internalization of the message, of passing it on and of co-operating in acting on it. He considers these effects to be the most important benefits of Child-to-Child. National evaluations of Child-to-Child activities in Uganda, Zambia, India and Botswana (see Chapter 1) have helped strengthen evidence in support of Child-to-Child, although more evidence is still needed. The case studies presented later in the book will also explore programme outcomes.

The need for greater clarity and agreement in defining the concept
The Child-to-Child concept is vulnerable because it lacks clear and

agreed definition. This problem is recognized by Hawes (1991): 'Some people claim the approach is a "catch-all", it is too woolly and wide and you can use it like the Bible to prove your--point on almost anything you want.' Consequently Child-to-Child can be difficult to explain succinctly to policy-makers and may be unattractive because it works through other programmes and so disguises ownership. Dissemination strategies need to be skilfully managed. They tend to be responsive and inter-sectoral, and do not fit easily into the project cycle favoured by most governments and agencies. It can also be difficult for those accustomed to an input/output model of education in schools and colleges to understand and accept benefits to the communicators of health activities not linked to a subject syllabus. There is another side to this, of course – it can also be argued that Child-to-Child is strong because it is an umbrella term.

Another concern is the way in which Child-to-Child has been narrowly interpreted in some programmes that are resistant to change: 'You get a large number of people like in a religion claiming they have got the word ... [they] have latched on to one element of Child-to-Child and will not hear of the others' (Hawes 1991). In some programmes children are known as 'little doctors' or 'little teachers'. These expressions give cause for concern where such programmes are informed by the traditional models of health and education, which Child-to-Child is trying to replace.

The risk of child exploitation Child-to-Child can be misunderstood and rather than leading to 'child power' it could lead to child exploitation. We saw earlier in this chapter that a gap very quickly opened between theory and practice, and concern has since increased about the extent to which misunderstandings and corruptions have been observed in practice. There are concerns that effective learning methods are being used to communicate incorrect health messages and that traditional didactic methods are being justified in the name of Child-to-Child. There is also concern where the principle of child involvement has been misinterpreted and becomes child exploitation, for example where children are used as megaphones for adult messages or are required to dig latrines in Child-to-Child programmes.

The gulf between theory and practice makes it all the more im-

---

What is Child-to-Child?

The encouragement and facilitation of the physical and psycho-social well-being of children by children, for themselves, their families and society.

It is:

Knowledge into action, child-centred, activity-oriented, enquiry-based.

It is not:

Competitive (it is non-judgemental), selective (all children should be included), oppressive (it is not authoritarian), compulsory.

It encourages personality development: self-esteem, self-reliance, critical thinking, interpersonal relationships, the development of values, sensitivity to others. It promotes improved quality of life: children's rights, socially appropriate behaviour, healthy living, ful-filled learning and giving. It recognizes that children are people too. It is applicable to children in all situations. It is holistic – a way of life.

Figure 4.6 What Child-to-Child is and what it is not (*source*: adapted from the report of a networking meeting on Child-to-Child in the southern states of India, 28 February to 2 March 1995).

portant to define more clearly what Child-to-Child is and what it is not (see Figure 4.6) There is now some agreement that central and non-negotiable to Child-to-Child are four cardinal principles:

- Child-to-Child involves children in useful and enjoyable activities appropriate to their age and ability.
- Child-to-Child develops partnerships for health at all levels, especially between health and education.
- Child-to-Child counts all children in.
- Child-to-Child does not belong to anyone.

Failure to recognize the realities of life The education systems of many countries are in crisis. Teachers are poorly trained, underpaid, overworked and demoralized. The curriculum is overcrowded, class sizes are large (frequently in excess of fifty children per class), buildings are dilapidated and there may be no latrines or water supply. Van der Vynckt (1992/3) has strongly lobbied for these realities to be given greater recognition in planning school health.

Child-to-Child depends on the willingness of teachers working under these difficult conditions to learn new skills and on their being able to develop sufficient competence and confidence to use them effectively with large classes of children. Effective facilitation of child-centred learning is more demanding of teachers' physical and intel-lectual energy than traditional didactic teaching. Insufficient attention has hitherto been accorded to issues of teacher supervision, support and reward for successful introduction of child-centred learning methodologies.

The importance of environmental (non-behavioural) barriers to behaviour change must not be underestimated. These barriers involve issues of access and equity in relation to economic, physical and service constraints and cast doubt on the extent to which health promotion on its own can improve health. The ability of children to make a difference must be viewed against the realities of life for children in many schools and communities.

The need to recognize how difficult it is to change minds In addition to these environmental barriers to the effectiveness of Child-to-Child there is the barrier presented by the innate conservatism of teachers who have been traditionally trained. Child-to-Child requires them to change the way they relate to children in the classroom, to become more flexible and to trust children and work alongside them as partners. Children are the least powerful members of most societies and, where the concept and its implications have been fully under-stood, the idea of 'child power' can be threatening to teachers, communities and governments alike. In some cultures there may be resistance to the notion of children researching community health issues. We need to question the extent to which practice and theory have corresponded and how far Child-to-Child has ever really been fully implemented. It can be argued that Child-to-Child is a dream in the minds of the theoreticians that has yet to come true (but it is not a very convincing argument).

The continuing influence of the 'former prophets' Child-to-Child owes
its origins and its development into a worldwide movement to the
vision and energy of a number of remarkable people. They themselves
have repeatedly insisted that Child-to-Child ideas have never been
their property, or a domain over which they should have some continuing control. But as we have seen, the respect in which these
'prophetic' figures are still held has not made it easy for them to fade
from the scene even when they have wished to do so. The weight of
their authority makes accurate balancing of the strengths and weaknesses of the Child-to-Child philosophy on its own merits more
difficult than would be the appraisal of a movement less associated
with its prime movers. In this respect it is clear that time will permit
a more detached and objective appraisal of Child-to-Child than is
now possible.

Note

1. Primary data are presented from structured inverviews with two
past directors of what is now the Child-to-Child Trust, Duncan Guthrie
and Hugh Hawes. Information has also come from informal discussions
with others who have been central to the inception of Child-to-Child
and to the development of its ideas (David Morley, John Webb, Otto
Wolff and Beverly Young).

5

Publications and Teaching Materials

In this chapter we establish a useful framework for evaluating the teaching–learning materials produced to support Child-to-Child activities. We then describe and analyse the range of materials currently in use, and examine the use of materials in selected sites around the world.

A Framework for Evaluating Child-to-Child Materials

The design and distribution of health education materials has been a major focus for the London-based Child-to-Child Trust. In the 'Review of Activities' published by the Trust in May 1996, the Trust described its three main functions:

> We design and distribute health education materials which are used by children, teachers and health workers; we advise and assist health and education workers in planning, implementing and evaluating Child-to-Child projects; we coordinate a worldwide information network for people and projects around the world who use the Child-to-Child approach.

The first function is further elaborated:

> Our materials are designed to teach people health education in an exciting way, using an approach which encourages them to participate actively in the process of learning and to put into practice what they learn. Most materials are copyright free and we encourage their translation and adaptation. (Child-to-Child 1996)

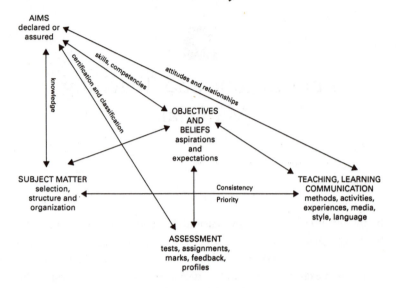

Figure 5.1 The curriculum model used at Sussex University
(*source*: Eraut et al. 1975)

It is against the criteria described in this function that we will review the materials used by Child-to-Child educators. To enable us to do this we shall use a popular curriculum model for analysing teaching–learning materials developed at Sussex University (Figure 5.1).

An important and useful characteristic of this model is the emphasis given to curriculum strategy – i.e. curriculum elements influencing decisions taken by practitioners when *using* teaching/learning materials. The focus of this model is therefore on evaluating 'patterns of use' of materials to be found in colleges and schools. In directing our attention at Child-to-Child materials it would seem important to look at the overall aims of the materials and then to examine them in relation to the four strategic components shown in the model: subject matter; objectives and outcomes; teaching–learning and communication methods; and assessment patterns. Before we do this it might be helpful to clarify what is meant by these terms (Figure 5.2).

The value of using a model such as this is that it helps us 'to focus on the key decisions which might be said to constitute a "curriculum

1. Subject matter	Chosen in preference to 'content', this term includes the organization and structuring of the content as well as its selection.
2. Teaching, learning and communication methods	A combination of methods and media with some consideration of design, style and language.
3. Assessment	This refers to the way in which a pupil, either explicitly or implicitly, is assessed.
4. Objectives and outcomes	Objectives refers to what is intended by the author of the materials; outcomes to what actually occurs when the materials are used. This seems to be particularly important in a situation where implicit objectives are not shared or understood by the practitioner.

Figure 5.2 Curriculum strategy

strategy", to see which decisions have already been taken and which are left open, where there is scope for modification and where there is none' (Eraut et al. 1975). From this general model we can generate a number of evaluation questions. For example:

- How do pupil and teacher materials fit together, and are there obvious points of conflict?
- In describing the coverage of subject matter in terms of knowledge, skills and attitudes, to what extent is the material explicitly concerned with the presentation of values or the development of attitudes?
- What knowledge and skills are needed by the pupils?
- How is the assessment related to pupil tasks (congruency?) and to the subject matter (uniformity of emphasis?).
- To what extent do the materials consist of factual materials, or do they try to communicate specific concepts, general concepts or principles?
- And finally, returning to Child-to-Child's own criterion: to what extent do the materials develop an active, practically oriented process of learning that is both instructive and exciting?

An Overview of Child-to-Child Materials

In this section we shall provide a general overview of the range of materials and then, using elements of the curriculum model described earlier, focus upon particular elements of the materials currently in use. The Child-to-Child literature published in English can be accessed through a review compiled by Richard Lansdown (1995). This account expands and updates three previous reviews (Feuerstein 1981; Somerset 1987; Heslop 1991) and provides a list of major work in other languages. The published literature comprises the following types of material:

- general training materials;
- materials aimed at the formal education system;
- publications about the Child-to-Child approach;
- publications by the Child-to-Child Trust of evaluations and major reports of programmes by Child-to-Child staff;
- publications by others commissioned by the Child-to-Child Trust, including reviews of activities and literature;
- publications about Child-to-Child by outside organizations that review or evaluate activities;
- reports and papers from international or regional meetings, conferences and workshops; and
- directories of activities undertaken by Child-to-Child lists of networks, partnerships, etc.

In the next section we shall look more closely at the training materials.

General training materials Lansdown (1995) points out that: 'From the outset the heart of the materials produced by Child-to-Child has been the Activity Sheets, leaflets which give basic information about a topic, along with ideas for projects and activities that can be carried out with children.' There are now approximately forty titles in eight categories, which have been collected together as the *Child-to-Child Resource Book Part Two* (1994b). Aimed at the teacher these sheets take a health education topic such as 'Our neighbourhood' and are structured around:

1. 'the idea', e.g. 'Children can take direct action to improve community health and welfare';
2. 'activities', e.g. 'mapping the community' or 'identifying health and safety needs'; and
3. 'follow-up' suggestions, which focus on what the children have learned and the impact of this learning upon the school and surrounding community.

Given the centrality of the Activity Sheets in the life and work of Child-to-Child, it is worth looking in more detail at an example. We shall give particular attention to the overall aims and to the teaching–learning and communications methods advocated. An example of a Child-to-Child Activity Sheet is given in Appendix 2.

The second major component of the general training materials are the Child-to-Child Readers. These books are published by major international publishing houses. As described by Colette Hawes (1993):

> The Child-to-Child Readers are story books with a health message. They give children *practice in easy reading*. They can be *read quickly* because their language is simple. The ideas and people in the books are *interesting* and the stories are *fun to read*. They encourage *reading for pleasure*. (original emphasis)

The Readers are written at three levels of reading difficulty, and their vocabulary ranges from about three hundred difficult words at Level 1 to about one thousand at Level 3. New and difficult words are carefully introduced and an effort is made to keep the story structure simple. Topics range from 'Good Food' (nutrition) at Level 1 to 'Deadly Habits' (smoking, alcohol and drug abuse; includes advice on AIDS prevention) at Level 3. The *Guide for Teachers* that accompanies the readers details ideas for teachers on how to develop the four language skills (reading, speaking, writing and listening) and suggests ways to extend the ideas into project and community work.

Other more general material produced by the Trust includes *Toys for Fun* (Carlisle 1988), published in six languages and showing how toys can be made from inexpensive materials; *We are on the Radio* (Hanbury and McCrum, undated), consisting of a booklet and an audio-tape, giving examples and ideas of ways in which health knowledge has been included in programmes made by children them-selves; and *Children for Health* (Hawes and Scotchmer 1993), a sub-stantial publication that develops the ideas of prime health messages originally set out in *Facts for Life* (UNICEF 1989) and relates the message to the Child-to-Child approach. Another recent publication, *Listening for Health* (Child-to-Child/ICCB 1997), aims to help adults understand more about listening and become better listeners, so that they can help children become better listeners and better health communicators. A training pack (Hanbury 1995) has been followed up with a training manual (Pridmore 1999) to help those running training courses.

Materials aimed at the formal education system Four substantial publications illustrate the importance Child-to-Child has accorded to working with, rather than in opposition to, the formal education system. The first, *Health into Mathematics* (Gibbs and Mutunga 1991), focuses on ways in which mathematics can be used to involve children in health activities. *Health into Science* similarly seeks to involve children in health activities through science. A companion volume, *Health into Social Studies*, is currently in preparation. The question of whether health education is best taught (or 'delivered') through such subjects or as part of a subject such as life skills or home economics or as a discrete subject on its own is one that is regularly addressed by those promoting the Child-to-Child approach.

Education for Health in Schools and Teachers' Colleges (Child-to-Child 1992) is a general introduction for those seeking guidance on how to plan health education in schools and colleges of education. Again the focus is on general principles, learning adaption and adoption to the reader. In *Health Promotion in Our Schools* (Hawes 1997) develops the concept of the 'Health Action School', arguing, along with WHO and UNICEF, that children can work with adults to make their learn-ing environments 'health-promoting' or 'health action' schools. This is an important publication as it moves the focus from the concept of 'child' to one of 'school'. It is also an indication that Child-to-Child has stopped looking inwards and begun to look outwards. Each September since 1995 the Child-to-Child Trust has run a 'Planning Health Promotion in Schools' course in London attended by health educational professionals from many different countries. In 1999 a course on inclusive education was launched. Linking the production of teaching/learning materials with training programmes continues to be a perceived role of the Trust. This role is replicated by a number of health education centres to be found in developing countries (e.g. CHETNA in India; the Childscope Network in Ghana).

Publications about Child-to-Child A number of important accounts have been published on the Child-to-Child movement since its inception in 1979. *Child-to-Child* (Aarons et al. 1979) is in some senses the bible of the Child-to-Child movement. As we saw in Chapter 3, this book is an output of the international seminar held in April 1978 involving 20 senior health educationists from 13 countries that first developed the Child-to-Child ideas. This book places emphasis upon the needs of poor countries, the role children can play in developing their own and their peers, health education, and the important role accorded the activity sheets. *Child-to-Child: Another Path to Learning* (Hawes 1988) usefully tells the story of Child-to-Child's development since the late 1970s. *Twelve Years On: A Child-to-Child Consultative Meeting* (Child-to-Child 1990) considers the position of the Trust twelve years after inception and discusses its future. The main points emerging from the consultative meeting give an idea of how the organization was changing at this time:

- a welcoming of the evolution of the Child-to-Child concept;
- an importance attached to integrating health messages with a wider movement; to promote health in the family and community
- the recognition of the potential of a Youth-to-Child programme;
- recommendation of action to promote Child-to-Child in Europe and North America;
- the identification of five programme priorities: (1) updating of Activity Sheets to address 'new' health concerns; (2) development of curriculum prototypes and guidelines; (3) extension of materials and activities from health to related environmental topics; (4) materials and activities emphasizing the role of Child-to-Child in growth and development, especially in the 0–3 age group; and (5) increased activities to meet the needs of 'marginalized' children;

- recommendation that the link between the Institutions of Child Health and Education in London remain strong;
- recommendation that the co-ordinating unit of the Trust in London should remain small; and
- recommendation that networking efforts promoting partnerships at international and national levels should be made.

If we look at these points six years further on we can see that considerable progress has been made, especially in three main areas of activity: 'Helping Children who Live in Difficult Circumstances', 'Improving Health Promotion in Schools' and 'Supporting the Development of Local Child-to-Child Resource Units' (Child-to-Child 1996). It is also interesting to see the extent to which the organization has maintained the tension between being true to its origins (by, for example, continued priority being accorded to the production of learning materials) while at the same time evolving to meet new challenges such as supporting global resource units and addressing the needs of children living in refugee camps and on the streets. The movement from the 'individual child' perspective to the 'school' also shows how the Trust is trying to keep abreast of changing needs and priorities through its publications and materials.

Evaluations and major reports of programmes by Child-to-Child staff and others commissioned by the Trust As we saw in Chapter 1, the Trust has produced two reviews or evaluations of its activities. Feuerstein (1981) reviewed information on activities submitted by 113 respondents in at least 57 countries and concluded that:

> Given the continued dedicated and often largely voluntary commitment of its practitioners and given the continued central supporting organization and the production of a diverse range of educational materials, it [Child-to-Child] will both continue to flourish and to expand.

In 1987 Tony Somerset conducted a follow-up survey. Questionnaires in English, French and Spanish were sent to 548 individuals associated with Child-to-Child projects. Of these 21 per cent (139 replies) were returned, from which 14 major conclusions were made.

This survey found that the Activity Sheets were the most popular materials available, with about two-thirds of respondents developing materials themselves. Another finding from this survey was that children's activities, especially in the community, needed to be reinforced by direct communication between the project initiators and the parents.

Papers given at major conferences Hawes and Morley (1988) review progress and the broadening concept of the approach from health education to better school practice and better school–community integration. Stephens (1993) reports on research-in-progress in Uganda and India, assessing the impact of Child-to-Child programmes on the educational life of schoolchildren in two clusters of schools.

Directories The Child-to-Child office in London acts as a co-ordinating centre and has produced a number of useful directories, such as *A Directory of Child-to-Child Activities in Tanzania* (1994) and *A Directory of Child-to-Child Activities Worldwide* (revised 1996).

An Analysis of Child-to-Child Materials

Aims An explicit aim of all the teaching–learning materials, and in particular the Activity Sheets, is the focus on empowering the child to act in the promotion of his or her own learning and in extending his or her actions to beyond the classroom walls. This 'child-centred' objective, which permeates the philosophy of the organization, raises a number of questions about the use of the materials.

The reality for many children in many poor countries is one in which schooling is characterized by a teacher-centred curriculum dominated by lack of material resources and an over-reliance upon examinations (see Hawes and Stephens 1990). The quality of the teacher and how he or she teaches (and often whether he or she turns up) has, therefore, to be recognized by an organization such as Child-to-Child. A result is that many of the materials, with the Readers being an exception, are targeted at the level of the classroom teacher for use with the children. A result of this has been the development of the Trust as an in-service training provider working alongside indigenous health educators. Since 1979 the Trust has worked tirelessly to motivate teachers and improve their skills in a large number of countries interested in improving the quality of their basic education system. Empowering the teacher, via materials and workshops, with an intention that he or she will, in turn, empower the child is a dilemma faced by many teacher educators. Implicitly, therefore, within many of the Child-to-Child materials is an adult focus, with the child regarded very much as the final beneficiary should the teaching be translated into learning.

Teaching, learning and communication methods An important methodological principle has been the development and promotion of teaching methods that are not only child-centred but link the classroom with the 'real world'. What Child-to-Child calls the 'Six Step Approach' emphasizes an enquiry-based approach in which children, often in groups, carry out project work – for example, doing surveys, visiting local health clinics – and return to the classroom to 'write up' and present their findings. This approach, which has dominated British primary education theory and practice since the 1960s, is now being questioned in Britain and elsewhere in the face of concern about low levels of literacy and numeracy, and recognition that in many countries teachers are unprepared professionally and in terms of resources to implement such an approach.

What we may in fact be seeing is a tension between the early idealistic aims of Child-to-Child and the realities of professional and cultural contexts where teaching is still characterized by what the teacher says and how well the child listens. A challenge for Child-to-Child in the development of its materials will be to take account of this tension and to continue to find ways to work within the paradox of empowering the teacher to do the same in turn for his or her pupils.

Pupil assessment The backwash effect of tests and examinations upon the curriculum is well known. A recent evaluation of the impact of Child-to-Child approaches upon the quality of primary schooling (Stephens 1997) in Uganda reveals another tension for teachers. This is the tension between recognizing the value in broadening the child's curriculum by, for example, encouraging more group and project work, and the need for children to perform well in the end-of-term and end-of-year examinations. At the micro-level of materials-in-use it can be argued that although the Activity Sheets and Readers excel in providing teachers with ideas, knowledge of content (i.e. the health messages), and activities that are engaging and focused upon community involvement, little guidance is given on ways to assess the impact of these activities upon the child's own development.

Although the 'follow-up' sections of the Activity Sheets offer ideas for ways to assess the general impact of Child-to-Child work, not enough attention is given to competencies, skills and knowledge to be developed by the child and to how these can be assessed and recorded. By giving prominence to the developmental role a child can play within the school and at home as an antidote to traditional chalk 'n' talk teaching, it may be that attention upon what the individual is actually learning while engaged in Child-to-Child activities has been neglected.

Objectives and outcomes If there is a 'gap' between what is intended by the Child-to-Child authors and the outcomes in classrooms and colleges around the world, such evidence will come from research, particularly that of a more qualitative kind, and from evaluation reports on the use or otherwise of Child-to-Child materials. Let us now consider this further.

Child-to-Child Materials: Evidence from the Field

In this section we shall look at evidence from three national settings – India, Zambia and Uganda – on how Child-to-Child materials have been implemented, and consider consequent issues raised for the improvement of teaching and learning more generally.

India UNICEF works closely with Child-to-Child in the Indian subcontinent. UNICEF has incorporated Child-to-Child materials in some of its programmes and also helped to fund Child-to-Child workshops in Bombay. Currently UNICEF is co-operating with the Central Health Education Bureau in incorporating materials and approaches

Objectives and emphasis

Child-centredness
Target audience
Children finding out (challenging)
The interest, variety and imaginative quality of activities
The evaluation and follow-up suggestions
How well does the Activity Sheet communicate?
Overall assessment of the Activity Sheet

Figure 5.3 The criteria developed by CHETNA for preparation
of Activity Sheets

into the large School Health Project in ten states. At a more local level, an active NGO, the Centre for Health Education, Training and Nutrition Awareness (CHETNA) based in Ahmadabad produces its own Activity Sheets. Their criteria in this task follow much of the inherent aims within the Child-to-Child programme (Figure 5.3).

Child-to-Child is also supported in India by the Aga Khan Foundation (AKF). In 1988 and 1993 its programmes were formally evaluated, and it is interesting to see to what extent the effectiveness of teaching–learning materials was assessed. In the 1988 evaluation, which focused on programmes developed at the Lady Irwin College in New Delhi, the evaluation reported that although most of the participating teachers found the Activity Sheets 'adequate' or useful as 'guidelines': 'four [of 43] of the teachers could not explain the use of the activity sheets whereas one teacher from the Janakpur school also reported reading aloud the activity sheets in the class. Two teachers reported reading aloud the activity sheets in class' (Sharma and Wadhwa 1988). As the evaluators conclude: 'This implies that correct usage of the activity sheets by the teachers should be ensured by the imple-mentors.'

The 1993 evaluation, which looked at a number of AKF-supported projects across India, had this to say about the teaching–learning materials:

Support materials are important, but should not be relied on to take the place of training. When Child-to-Child was initiated, one of the first things produced was a set of Activity Sheets, which was to be used by teachers to help them plan how they would work with children around the various health topics. The Activity Sheets were usually introduced to teachers early on in their training. Their purpose would be clarified and the various components discussed. One of the key tasks during training was for teachers to create their own Activity Sheets. Consistently, in all the AKF-funded projects, teachers used the Activity Sheets they created in the workshops, but almost always found fault with those produced on a mass scale, even those that had been produced in India.

The usefulness of materials is determined by the teachers' attitudes towards them. As Bruner states:

> Teachers can make or break materials by their attitude toward them and their pedagogical procedures – often more implicitly than explicitly. No matter how well the material may be presented by the curriculum maker, it may be over the head of teacher and student alike, producing in the end a misconception. (1977: 166)

To sum up: good materials cannot stand on their own, but they can provide good models. It was an important part of their learning for teachers to go through the process of creating their own Activity Sheets and teaching aids. It was one of the best ways of getting them to understand what it was they were meant to be doing within Child-to-Child. What that may mean is that teachers are unlikely spontaneously to pick up an Activity Sheet and use it. Without training and a supportive context, Activity Sheets probably have little value (Evans 1993).

Zambia   Child-to-Child was launched in Zambia in 1986 with encouragement from President Kenneth Kaunda. Ten years later the programmes were evaluated by a consultant, Jennifer Chiwela. She has this to say about the materials in use:

> More than 60% of Child-to-Child schools received the relevant Child-to-Child resource materials such as Children for Health and the WASHE Green Folder. The situation found in schools was that
>
> - about 50% of teachers from schools which received resource materials were in possession of them but needed help on their usage;

- about 50% of teachers from schools which received resource materials had no regular access to them as they were being kept by the school administration;
- about 30% of the schools visited had seen neither the Children for Health book nor the WASHE Green Folder. (Chiwela 1996)

She does not elaborate on what help teachers needed in their usage, but in an earlier section of the evaluation discusses the problem of teachers integrating Child-to-Child activities into their syllabus-dominated classroom work.

Zambia is also a country in which much good work has been achieved at teachers' college level. In 1992 teacher educators from four African countries – Sierra Leone, Zambia, Kenya and Uganda – met in Nairobi to learn from the experience of introducing Child-to-Child in their respective colleges and primary schools. The Zambian team painted a reasonably positive picture, emphasizing the importance in adapting imported materials for local use:

Activity Sheets produced internationally by Child-to-Child are used regularly in training course at central level, and by curriculum planners together with the books Primary Health Education and Health into Mathematics. All are considered relevant and useful. The Child-to-Child readers have been distributed to small numbers of schools and have received a warm reception. They have been particularly commended by the English Language Division in the Curriculum Development Centre. However, numbers available have always been relatively small and neither the readers nor the sheets have been widely used in the colleges or associated schools. Although the sheets are copyright-free, local reproduction costs are high.

Locally generated materials have also been produced in some quantity. An excellent resource book, *Child-to-Child in Zambia*, was produced in 1987 by the Institute for Christian Leadership together with a set of wall charts. These were distributed in reasonable numbers but attempts to finance their distribution in bulk were not successful. As a result of writing workshops and the outcomes of centrally organized training there is now a considerable bank of useful locally produced materials for teachers. However, owing to time constraints and printing difficulties these have still to reach the colleges and schools. Meanwhile the decentralization of Child-to-Child activity to school and community level has resulted in the emergence of a large amount of useful material (much of it in local languages) in the form of plays, songs, and stories. It is the policy of Child-to-Child Zambia to collect these in resource centres based on teachers' colleges and to make them available at district and community level. (Hawes 1992)

Uganda Like Zambia and India, Uganda has an established Child-to-Child programme working at college and school level. The School Health Education Project (SHEP), which is an inter-sectoral project approach to health education in Uganda through schools, has been collaborating with Child-to-Child since its creation in 1986 in the production of books for teachers and pupils, kits on water and sanitation, control of diarrhoeal disease, immunization and AIDS. At the 1992 Nairobi seminar the following evaluation of materials at national and local levels was offered:

> *Child-to-Child Materials at National Level* While materials emanating from SHEP and from Child-to-Child in London have been extremely useful the project organizers have been very aware of the need to produce local materials. Thus in addition to newsletters, calendars, leaflets and other printed materials, Child-to-Child Uganda has now produced a video of its activities, both for national and international viewing.
>
> *Child-to-Child Materials at Local Level* Crafts – At local level (colleges and schools) continual attempts are made to stimulate the production of craft work to aid health, e.g. brooms, pots, covers, racks, containers for rubbish.
>
> • Collection of local songs, poems and stories.
> • Toys and play materials for children. Competitions and displays help to create awareness and friendly rivalry in the production of materials. (Hawes 1992)

Conclusion

The purpose of this chapter has been to review and assess the effectiveness of Child-to-Child publications and teaching–learning materials. Particular attention has been paid to a model of analysis which looks at materials in use as part of a curriculum strategy involving the interplay between key elements: aims, objectives and outcomes, teaching–learning methods, subject matter, and assessment patterns. A wide array of curriculum guides, 'how to' documents, and teaching–learning materials have been generated by the Child-to-Child Trust and by groups of activists, often working within local NGOs in the so-called developing world. Much of this wealth of material has been appreciated by teachers and students working within schools and colleges. Cheap, teacher-friendly, copyright-free, and sometimes translated into local languages, the materials can be found in use in many national settings.

A critique of how these methods are used in three national contexts reveals a number of important concerns:

- that teaching–learning materials produced by the Trust are essentially teacher-centred and require training to assist users in developing child-centred pedagogies;
- that for effective use materials must be 'processed' by the teachers so that rather than being complementary to lesson plans, etc., they become integrated and 'owned' by the teachers;
- that the issue of children's learning and ways of effectively measuring assessment of learning is built into the support materials; and
- that more attention be given to supporting the production of local materials guided by those emanating from London and elsewhere.

III

Case Studies of Child-to-Child in Action around the World

6

Learning from Children in India, Mexico and the United Kingdom

In this chapter, and in the next three chapters, we shall look at case studies of Child-to-Child from around the world. Each case study will provide information on the social, political and economic context in which the programme has been developed, explain how it was started and has been kept going and describe how Child-to-Child ideas have been adapted to the particular context. Any outcomes of the programme are also reported and the influences, problems and constraints that have affected the programme are identified. Strategies are explored for overcoming difficulties and moving the programme forward.

A Review of Child-to-Child Activities of the Save the Children Fund (UK) in Nepal

Nepal ranks as one of the poorest nations in the world, with a GNP of $200 (UNICEF 1997). Basic government health services are meagre or unavailable to the majority of the population, which is rural. The poor health of children is further undermined by chronic malnutrition owing to their families' poverty and lack of health awareness. Of the 62 per cent of children enrolled in school, only 27 per cent complete five years of primary schooling. Of those enrolled, only 31 per cent are girls.

Save the Children Fund (SCF) introduced, in 1989, the Child-to-Child approach to health promotion in schools as an outreach activity of the MCH (maternal and child health) clinics, wherein children became communicators of health messages to other children, families and the community. By 1997 the programme had expanded to 50 schools. In 1995, SCF incorporated the promotion of children's rights into the Child-to-Child programme. This review came at a critical juncture in SCF's country programme development as its strategic focus moved from health delivery to a broader mandate for the promotion of children's rights. The key objectives of the review were therefore to assess (a) the quality and impact of the Child-to-Child activities in the context of SCF's health programming; and (b) the potential of the Child-to-Child approach to contribute to the realization of children's rights.

Study methods Schools from two of SCF's programme areas were selected, representing contrasting models of implementation. The Sindhupalchowk schools initiated a Child-to-Child health programme in 1989 and the Surkhet schools initiated Child-to-Child activities with emphasis on child rights in 1995. A small sample of Child-to-Child schools from the programme areas was contrasted with control schools.

The review was qualitative, ensured involvement of all stakeholders – adults and children – and was evolved with the full participation of SCF policy and programme staff. Child-centred Participatory Research Techniques (PRA) such as drawing, mapping, time trends and process plotting were devised to focus on the views and experiences of children. Data generated were also differentiated on gender. Researchers observed Child-to-Child activities, interviewed and had focus group discussions with parents, teachers, school management committees, women's groups, out-of-school children, local/district education officials and MCH workers, to ensure the triangulation of findings.

Child-to-Child as a health programme The Sindhupalchowk schools adopted the Child-to-Child approach to provide health education for Standards I to V. SCF staff, and later teachers, gave clearly stated messages on health and hygiene to children, who were then expected to pass them on to their families, friends and the community at large. The messenger role of children was reinforced and strengthened through planned family and community linkage.

What worked The Child-to-Child programme had clearly impacted on children's health knowledge, attitudes and behaviour in contrast to children in control schools. There was improvement in personal, home and school cleanliness, school attendance and communication skills of children, and enhanced leadership roles for girls were clearly evident. The development of linkages with community groups – e.g. mothers' groups, non-formal education (NFE) groups and school management committees – ensured a supportive environment for children's action, as well as improving the school infrastructure and quality of school management. However, in terms of children's participation, the Sindhupalchowk model was essentially teacher-directed and use of creative communication methods (drama, games, etc.) was limited.

Child-to-Child and promotion of children's rights In the Surkhet schools, by contrast, the Child-to-Child six-step active learning approach was adopted to promote the concept of children's participation in decision-making. At each step, children were to take the lead in identifying, prioritizing and finding solutions to health problems. Teachers were trained in this participatory, more child-centred approach.

What worked Although children's health knowledge and hygiene practices had improved in the Surkhet Child-to-Child schools (in comparison with the control school), the differences were less sharp than in Sindhupalchowk. Teachers had difficulty in implementing the six-step approach that promoted children's participation as they found it time-consuming and were not convinced about children's capabilities in assuming decision-making roles.

Lessons learned In contrasting the lessons learned from the two models, it is clear that a successful implementation of the Child-to-Child approach is dependent upon:

- the degree of the teacher's belief in the capacity of children to participate and take effective, self directed action;
- the extent of children's self-esteem and communication skills; and

- the degree of support for children's proactive role from parents and community.

The Child-to-Child approach to health promotion provides a practical, acceptable process towards children's right to participate in decisions affecting their lives. This review recommends the phasing of implementation in the government schools in Nepal to promote quality and sustainability. The initial phase may be modest, as in the Sindhupalchowk model, where children are given opportunities to be messengers of health information and, in this way, build in themselves, their families, schools and communities an essential acceptance and confidence about children's capabilities. It may then be more feasible to move on to an ambitious Child-to-Child model of full participation by children, where adults play a less directive and more facilitative role.

Niño a Niño (Child to Child) in Oaxaca, Mexico

Oaxaca and its children   Oaxaca state is situated on the Pacific coast in the south-west of the Mexican Republic. It shares its borders with Chiapas, Guerrero, Puebla, and Veracruz. Oaxaca enjoys great diversity in indigenous cultures. More than 18 different ethnic groups, 14 different languages and 44 dialects are recognized in the state. However, the majority of the adult population and pre-school population are fluent only in their native tongues.

In spite of its cultural diversity and rich natural resources, Oaxaca is one of the poorest states in the republic. Continuous deforestation has resulted in the land between the two mountain ranges being considered semi-arid and water is increasingly a major problem for the majority of the Oaxacan people, not only for their own personal consumption, but also for the maintenance of their crops and animals. In areas where the land is still fertile, the fruit and vegetables produced are mostly exported. Local farmers are left with the poorest land and crops. Currently, the main industries for Oaxaca are tourism and artistry, and export cash-crops such as coffee, timber, fruits and vegetables. As the population continues to grow, the land can no longer sustain entire families and many people have moved to the larger cities within Oaxaca or to Mexico City. The rate of migration from the *pueblos* (villages) to the cities grows continually, and many men migrate to the United States for two or three years at a time to maintain their families in Oaxaca, leaving the women and young children alone to mind the farms and their families.

According to the State Council on Population, 60 per cent of the Oaxacan people continue to live in their rural villages of origin, of which 50 per cent are inaccessible by roads, leaving the inhabitants virtually out of reach, particularly in regard to health care, education, electricity, and potable water services. Fifty per cent of the state's total population of approximately 3 million have no access to any health services. Forty-three per cent of the population is younger than 15 years of age, of whom 98 per cent live in the indigenous rural communities. There is a 10 per cent infant mortality rate, usually a result of malnutrition, infectious diseases, gastro-intestinal infections leading to dehydration, respiratory illnesses, and accidents; all of these are easily preventable.

Mexico is politically controlled by the Institutional Revolutionary Party (PRI), which has been 'democratically' voted into power for the past 71 years. There is a great deal of political unrest and military activity, particularly in the rural areas, and a growing national consciousness of the need for change.

Getting started   Niño a Niño was initiated in Oaxaca in 1990 through the efforts of a group of dedicated individuals. Two basic courses were run in the first year to train local people from various indigenous communities to work as 'guides' with the children in their communities. At that time, the only criterion for selecting people to become guides was that they should have a genuine interest in working with the children. As a result, there was an extremely wide variety of participants on the training courses in terms of their basic education, and understanding of health education and community development. There was an equally wide range of cultural and language backgrounds.

Between 1990 and 1994, two 14-day courses were offered each year to train more guides. Several techniques were presented through which the guides could work with the children to select, study, act upon and evaluate their topics. These techniques included the use of drama, songs and games with simple health messages, puppetry, painting, clay modelling, and local resources such as gourds used to demonstrate how a child dehydrates.

The guides were trained to lead their children through the Child-to-Child methodology. They would help the children to (i) recognize a health problem; (ii) study that problem; (iii) act to prevent that problem; and (iv) evaluate their work and the results of their actions. Finally, as an integral part of the course, the trainee guides had the opportunity to put into practice what they were learning with a group of local schoolchildren.

Beginning in 1991, three-day evaluations were regularly hosted in the city of Oaxaca to enable the guides who had been actively working with children to share their experiences of how the programme was working in their communities, discuss their successes and problems, and explore solutions. By 1995 it became clear that as the programme expanded there were not enough people or financial resources at the centre in Oaxaca City to manage the programme effectively. This resulted in a poor understanding of how the programme was working in the communities. As a consequence, a systematic project planning and evaluation schedule was devised and financial support actively sought.

Development of the programme What started out as Niño a Niño, Oaxaca has since become Niño a Niño Mexico. There are now groups of children in six states throughout the republic – Oaxaca, Chiapas, Campeche, Quintana Roo, Querétaro and Guanajuato – and in Mexico City. A staff comprising 75 guides and six regional co-ordinators works with approximately 1,500 children who in turn reach out to over 3,000 children.

The expansion of the programme has resulted in a number of changes being implemented:

1. Administrative changes have included: the hiring of full-time Mexican staff to co-ordinate the various activities to develop the necessary materials and to visit communities; and the training of six regional co-ordinators to serve as a link between the com-

munities and the central office in Oaxaca City, and provide further support to the guides and children. These regional co-ordinators are also responsible for hosting basic courses and guides' and children's meetings at the regional level.

2. The organization has become a legally recognized NGO with tax-exempt status, which is very important for the future of Niño a Niño in securing economic stability with a Mexican base.

3. There is a board of directors, which includes members of Oaxaca's 'sister city', Palo Alto in California, as well as Dr Tenorio, one of the original founders of Niño a Niño.

4. There have been adjustments to the programme of activities, shifting priorities from general growth and increasing numbers of groups to strengthening and supporting existing groups and guides. One basic course is offered each year (only in regions where Niño a Niño is already working). In areas where the guides are in need of help, the number of gatherings and/or training sessions has been increased. Evaluative visits to communities, which have involved meetings with parents and town authorities, have become an integral part of the programme.

5. The organization hosts annual regional gatherings of children in which 100–125 children from within a region get together for three days to share experiences and learn about a theme, previously selected by the children.

Adapting theory to practice The most striking feature of the organization in Oaxaca is that it is strictly community based. With the exception of one group, Niño a Niño does not function within the public educational system or the governmental health programmes. The positive aspect is the flexibility of the programme and the dedication of the guides, all of whom are volunteers and are very dedicated to the programme, to the children with whom they work and to the improvement of their communities. The negative aspect is that Niño a Niño does not have an 'automatic' infrastructure within which to work and/or to rely upon for support, educated personnel, materials, salaries, etc. Thus, as noted above, they are in the process of designing their own infrastructure, unique to Child-to-Child in Mexico.

It must be noted that the flexibility of the children in their work is a major advantage. Niño a Niño emphasizes the importance of developing the children's life skills, those needed to constructively criticize their surroundings, to be creative and solve problems, and to work together, allowing each person to contribute his or her particular gift. Within the Mexican public school system, this is virtually impossible as the teachers are in tight control.

Many of the materials and suggested techniques published by the Child-to-Child Trust are in use. Niño a Niño has also created many materials specific to the needs of their Child-to-Child groups and has sought ways to utilize the resources available in their communities. In addition, it has created materials specific to the needs of the guides, recognizing that the guides are also products of the very formal educational system and need continued support in order to feel free to break with the customary hierarchical structure.

Currently, Niño a Niño is designing a very specific project in nutrition for all groups. The project encompasses monitoring the families involved, the children's growth and weight patterns, basic education in nutrition, composting and the care of family gardens, and the preparation of more nourishing meals.

Influences, problems and constraints As a developing organization, Niño a Niño has faced significant challenges:

1. By overlooking the need to set the selection criteria for 'guides', i.e. a primary education with some basic health knowledge, more training and support than anticipated have been required.
2. When the programme was initiated, there was no concern for where it would be implemented. As a result, Niño a Niño is spread out rather thinly and has active communities in five of the seven regions of Oaxaca, with many communities inaccessible by road, and the majority without any regular phone or mail system. Thus communication has been, and continues to be, a major problem. Time and transport constraints in visiting the various communities have been similarly problematic. These notwithstanding, expansion proceeds and Niño a Niño continues to reach virgin communities.
3. The lack of formative evaluation in the early years has resulted in the need for the active guides to be retrained so that they can use the materials and resources available to them more effectively.

4. The strict reliance upon volunteers in all aspects of the programme has been difficult. It has become clear that in order for the programme to be implemented successfully, paid staff are required to provide the necessary follow-up support and training.

5. The Child-to-Child philosophy is very much a revolutionary approach to education in Mexico. It has been a double challenge to change the way of thinking of the guides involved, as well as that of the children. Further, the application of children's learning in practice has presented difficulties as it has involved changes in the way parents relate to their children and has challenged the community to view them as playing an active role in community life.

6. Prior to the establishment of Niño a Niño as a legal entity problems arose due to the inability to develop a sound financial basis. The programme receives only a small amount of funding from a Catholic organization based in North America and needs to raise further funding. The current aim is to attain a higher degree of economic stability to secure the future of Niño a Niño in Mexico.

The co-ordinating team, based in a small central office in Oaxaca City, has worked strenuously to overcome these difficulties. Fortunately the members of the team have now worked together for the past two and a half years to help develop the current structures and programmes. This very dedicated team intends to remain together for a few more years in order to realize their current vision.

Shared Learning in Action: Child-to-Child Experience from the United Kingdom

Merseyside and its children   The Child-to-Child approach was first used in schools in the borough of Merseyside, an area in the north-west of England, in 1991. Merseyside is an area of high unemployment and has a range of associated social problems. The number of single parents is higher than the national average and there is a disproportionately high incidence of illnesses such as heart disease and lung cancer, which are lifestyle-related (Liverpool Public Health Annual Report 1995).

Getting started Awareness of the social and health needs of its school population prompted Knowsley Local Education Authority in Merseyside to seek innovative strategies to address such important issues as smoking and drug misuse among school-age children. The Authority decided to support the Child-to-Child approach in schools under its jurisdiction and initially the approach was introduced by the programme director (Sue Occleston) into one school, where the focus was on smoking prevention. Following the successful experience of this 'pilot', the approach was used in Merseyside to pursue other issues. It soon became apparent, however, that the nature of community health issues differs from those for which Child-to-Child materials have been designed in developing countries. For example, nutrition issues are concerned with media influences on eating habits rather than access to a variety of foods.

In designing projects on nutrition, environmental health hazards, drug abuse, bullying, crime prevention and safety, Child-to-Child ideas and methods have been used to develop an approach called 'Shared Learning in Action'. This approach places special emphasis on building up children's self-esteem and developing the life skills needed for responsible citizenship and resisting peer group pressure. Through working with children using this approach, adults can increase their awareness of how children perceive their community and come to recognize that children are not 'empty vessels' to be filled with information but have their own repository of information and opinions, which are of potential benefit to the entire community. Inherent in the approach is an understanding that children's participation in the community is integral to citizenship education. Participation helps children to acknowledge their membership of the community and its associated rights and responsibilities. It also enables them to recognize their ability to influence the world around them and to value their unique contribution, and increases their self-esteem. Shared Learning in Action programmes have utilized resources already available in schools and communities as well as developing new materials.

Developing the programme Schoolteachers and adult volunteers (mostly parents) have been involved through training and/or participation in activities with children. This has enabled them to develop a range of skills, which can further their own educational opportunities and also enhance their employment potential in an area where there is high unemployment. The acquisition of skills has also served to strengthen relationships and thus consolidate their own community. Parents involved in the programme have proved to be very open to listening to children, especially when invited into the school for programme activities. Developing partnerships is a major component of the approach, and 'experts' such as school nurses and police officers are encouraged to respond to children's initiatives and participate in and support school health activities. In the course of the children's research activities children may interview such 'experts', thereby assuming some control of the project.

Adapting theory to practice   Health education is one of the five cross-curricular themes identified within the National Curriculum for schools in the United Kingdom. These themes do not form part of the core curriculum but should be integrated across core curriculum subjects. While some health issues can be addressed in core subjects such as science, teachers need support and encouragement to ensure that health issues receive adequate attention. In Merseyside the Shared Learning in Action approach has been used to develop programmes in relation to three cross-curricular themes: health education (smoking, drugs, food choices); environment (hazards, safety); and citizenship (crime prevention, bullying). The approach can also be implemented in many of the core subjects, such as English.

This analysis of the health issues identified by schools also demonstrates how the majority of health issues in the United Kingdom are commonly regarded as being 'lifestyle'-related. Drug misuse and associated problems such as crime are pressing problems for schools, professionals and the wider community. It is therefore important to tackle the issue of crime prevention together with drug misuse. Parents' willingness to give freely of their time as volunteers and to be involved in activities related to drug education demonstrates the level of their concern.

As mentioned above, the raising of self-esteem is a fundamental aim of Shared Learning in Action. The approach recognizes that self-esteem and the relationships between members of the peer group are critical determinants of behaviour. For example, when schoolchildren in Merseyside were asked why a person of their age might smoke, the most frequent responses were: peer pressure and the desire to look 'cool', 'tough', 'big', to be 'noticed' or to emulate adults. In order to build self-esteem children have been involved in activities that develop their skills in decision-making and communication and teach the values inherent in responsible citizenship. The methods employed are participatory. Small group work is emphasized since it enables children to develop skills in negotiation and collaboration. Children participate in games that explore their feelings and engage in discussion that opens channels of communication on issues of peer influence and its effects on behaviour. Many methods are used to facilitate discussion, such as questioning, pictures, drawing or role-play. The aim is to help children to understand their feelings better and to see what it is that influences their feelings and how this impacts on behaviour. The key to success is the expert support offered by the project team and crucially, the support of trained adults (usually parents) in the classroom.

Shared Learning in Action has mainly been used in the primary school setting with children aged nine to eleven years of age and with older children in secondary schools in 'Personal and Social Education' lessons. It has been used successfully with groups of children and young people in the community setting, for example youth groups and after-school clubs. It has the potential for wider application. The training provided for teachers, health workers and other professionals varies according to their background and experience, but always includes an introduction to the history and underlying philosophy of the approach, the methodology, methods and classroom management strategies.

Problems and constraints Initially there was a major problem convincing teachers that the approach would work, that it could be done in their schools. This was overcome by providing teachers with continued support following the initial training, especially when they first tried involving children in the activities. The support took the form of the programme director visiting the school, working alongside the teacher in the classroom and being available to discuss what went well and what did not. It was also important to allow the more able teachers to be creative within the step-by-step framework provided by the methodology. The framework helped less able teachers by giving them a structure to work within which helped them to plan their lessons.

Another critical issue was how to fit the Shared Learning and Action approach into the National Curriculum as a cross-curricular issue. Due to perceived time constraints such issues tend to get squeezed out, and Shared Learning and Action needs time for children to be involved in the active learning methods. This problem was addressed through discussion with teachers to raise awareness of the way in which the approach both fulfils and enhances existing curriculum needs in that it provides an opportunity for children to practise important skills. For example, in English, the need for children to develop communications skills such as listening, speaking and writing is a priority. Once teachers understood that the approach could be used as a vehicle for these skills they were more likely to adopt it.

In some schools teachers and parents initially had reservations about the extent to which children were able to make decisions and take action for health. Working around drugs education helped to overcome this problem as the approach helped them to recognize that children often had more knowledge and experience than they themselves did and were able to make good decisions.

Evaluation and training Evaluation of Shared Learning in Action has involved all the key players: professionals, parents and children. Teachers have affirmed the value inherent in the transferable nature of the facilitation skills they have gained through working in a more participatory way with children. Health workers and other professionals have endorsed the importance of enabling children to develop participatory and decision-making skills. Parents have reported that their improved ability to communicate with children about issues such as drug misuse was important to them, and that they felt proud of what the children could do. Both teachers and adult volunteers have reported an increase in their confidence in children and a creation or strengthening of links between the school and community, which has led to greater understanding and empathy between previously polarized groups such as the elderly and youth.

It must be acknowledged, however, that in the few situations where the approach has been evaluated less favourably teachers were uncertain about the capacity of children to make decisions and implement them.

One indicator of the success of the approach is the continued funding it is attracting from a variety of donor agencies. The United Kingdom Home Office has funded a community and schools drugs prevention project; the European Union has funded a smoking prevention project with partners in the United Kingdom, France and Portugal; and the Save the Children Fund has initiated training and projects in Canada with the Inuit and aboriginal communities.

Conclusion

Shared Learning in Action has proved to be a useful and manageable approach for teachers working with children in school contexts in the United Kingdom. It can assist teachers by giving them a structured framework through which to facilitate real opportunities for children to participate in decision-making, to have their ideas listened to, and to take action. It can be an effective approach in that it gives children and young people the opportunity to participate freely, while providing a structure that offers guidance and a framework to any project. The approach has been used to explore many issues of interest to children and young people. Once practitioners understand the nature of the powerful educational process implicit in the approach, they are able to transfer the skills they have learned to a variety of issues. The interest already shown in Shared Learning in Action indicates that the activities will continue to grow and extend to other settings, such as preschools. There is also further scope for follow-up work with primary schoolchildren to develop the approach to meet their future needs.

7

Learning from Children in Africa

The CHILD-to-Child Little Teacher Programme in Botswana

Botswana is a large (582,000 sq. km) landlocked country in southern Africa. Roughly half of its very small population (1.3 million in 1991) live in crowded urban areas and the other half in the sparsely populated rural areas. Since independence from British rule in 1966 the economy has enjoyed one of the highest rates of growth in sub-Saharan Africa. Expansion in the area of formal schooling has been enormous, and 85 per cent of primary school-age children now attend school. However, over one-half of all households are living in poverty, and lack food and economic security. Droughts are frequent and malnutrition has been reduced in recent years only by extensive drought relief feeding and employment interventions.

Getting started The CHILD-to-child Little Teacher Programme was started in 1979 as an outreach programme in two pilot schools to make a practical contribution to the International Year of the Child. It aimed to teach and encourage primary schoolchildren to concern themselves with the health, welfare and development of their younger brothers and sisters and of other young children in the community. Schoolteachers responsible for implementing the programme taught the primary schoolchildren who, it was hoped, would then carry the messages to younger children at home or in the community who had not yet started school. The younger children were simply called 'students'. This scheme was rapidly modified. By 1981 preschool

125

children were attending school regularly and taking part in activities with primary schoolchildren supervised by the schoolteachers, who were known as CHILD-to-child teachers. This was the most important change to have been made to the original scheme. Somerset (1987: 78) notes that the use of the terms 'little teacher' for the primary schoolchildren and 'preschooler' for the preschool children is a more recent innovation.

Developing the programme Every year since the inception of the programme four schools, deemed to be most in need of the programme, have been selected by the co-ordinator of the CHILD-to-child Network together with a representative of the Ministry of Education. The co-ordinator writes to the head teacher of each school through the district education officer to invite that school to participate. She then visits the school to explain to the head teacher what the programme involves and what it offers to the children. If the teachers are interested there is a meeting with representatives from the parent–teacher association (PTA), the village development committee and any NGOs working in that area in community development. The final commitment to participate in the programme is made at a meeting at the chief's meeting house (*kgotla*). Support for the programme is thereby gained at the outset through a process of wide consultation before it is officially launched in the presence of pupils, teachers, parents and important members of the community. Two teachers are selected to be CHILD-to-child teachers in the school, and they attend a workshop to learn about the programme and how to run it. The CHILD-to-child Network agrees to provide the lesson plans, paper, crayons and paints, to arrange visits by the co-ordinator at least four times a year to provide support for the teachers and to monitor the programme, and to hold annual workshops where teachers can share experiences and learn more about the programme. The Ministry of Education provides encouragement but the small amount of funding needed is raised entirely by the CHILD-to-child Network. Through this process 56 schools had joined the programmes by 1996 and it was estimated that since the programme started more than 700 primary school teachers and 50,000 children had been involved in it.

Adapting theory to practice   The notion of older children helping younger children is part of the traditional pattern of early childhood socialization in Botswana, and consequently CHILD-to-child can be considered to be at home within the culture. However, this is not the whole story. Although the notion of children helping children appears to be highly acceptable, the notion of children passing on ideas to their parents is more problematic, conflicting as it does with cultural norms, family characteristics and the child's position and status within the family. In Botswana children promoting health to their elders goes against the tradition of wisdom being passed down from the older to the younger within a strongly hierarchical social structure. Similarly, the notion of partnership with children is also problematic in view of the low position children occupy in the social hierarchy. It is not surprising, therefore, that in adapting theory to practice the Little Teacher Programme focuses on what older children can do to introduce school readiness skills such as hygiene and nutrition to preschoolers (Masolotate 1997).

Let us now look more closely at school-based CHILD-to-child sessions. Pridmore (1996) presents data from classroom observation to show how the style of implementation varies between schools. She describes the process in a rural school where six teachers had volunteered to run the Little Teacher Programme and had been doing so for more than a decade. These teachers worked together in pairs to run a session, although all teachers were present at each session. Little Teacher sessions took place three times a week in the middle of the afternoon after classes had finished for the day. At the beginning of the session the teachers gathered under a large tree in the dusty school compound together with child educators and preschoolers. The session started with singing and an energetic game, which involved everyone standing in a large circle while children ran races around the circumference. After this the preschoolers were released to play on their own for a short while.

One of the schoolteachers then stood in front of the group of child educators seated on the ground and talked to them for about fifteen minutes. These children were then sent to find their preschool 'twins' and take them to join one of the schoolteachers. (They were free to choose which teacher they wanted to be with.) In this way each of the six schoolteachers was responsible for about half a dozen child educators and their preschool 'twins'. Each child educator then spent 15 minutes passing the message to their preschooler. When they thought the message had been learned they took the preschooler to the schoolteacher, who checked that the preschooler could repeat the message. The whole group then came back together and the process was repeated from the beginning. The other teacher responsible for the session gave her presentation and the children then divided into the six smaller groups, each group supervised by a schoolteacher. The session finished with more singing and another group game.

When asked whether the children took home the messages taught in these sessions, the schoolteachers were all agreed that they did. They contended that this success was due to the community being fully engaged with the programme, with parents frequently coming to the school to talk about what their children had been doing in the programme. Their views were supported by the observation during field visits that parents were always present and helping in this school. In discussion with the researcher parents were very positive about child educators helping preschoolers to learn, but there was no mention of its value to the older children.

Programme evaluation   Aspects of the programme have been evaluated by Somerset (1987), Babugura et al. (1993) and Pridmore (1996). In 1993 UNICEF commissioned the Botswana Educational Research Foundation (BERA) to conduct an evaluation of the Little Teacher Programme. As we saw in Chapter 1 the evaluation report (Babugura et al. 1993) stated that teachers were 'emphatic' that the programme made a positive difference in preparing children for primary schooling, but parents and community groups were not involved as much as had been hoped and ongoing evaluation by the programme implementers had been only partial.

A small controlled study conducted by Pridmore (1996) concluded that 'little teachers' appeared to have had a significant effect on the ability of preschoolers to recall health messages, and that performing the role of a little teacher resulted in a significant increase in their own ability to recall health messages. Most of the messages in the intervention programme were passed by girls to their mothers (or other female relative) in the home. This was an important finding of this study and supports the findings of Zaveri in India (1988: 208). However, the study also found that parents often do not have the time to listen to their children even if they want to, and that space needs to be made available for parents and children to come together and communicate. The frequent absence of fathers was found to be an important factor, making it difficult for children to pass messages to their fathers.

The study found that the acceptability of children as educators of their younger siblings was not in doubt, whereas the notion of children as educators of parents was problematic. The results suggested that, although children had been able to pass some of the intervention messages to their parents, other types of message would be more difficult for them to pass. Messages about hygiene and about child growth and development were found to be equally acceptable, whereas messages about, for example, how long a child should be breastfed – which could imply lack of respect for parental experience – would be rejected. It was regarded as very important that children should approach adults in a respectful manner. Furthermore, messages that carried resource implications, such as money to buy soap for hand washing, might not be well received. There was some evidence, however, that the reticence that parents have traditionally felt about discussing sexual health with their children is beginning to decrease because parents recognize that children need to be informed if they are to help prevent the spread of infections such as HIV. These findings highlighted the difficulties faced by children in passing messages to adults in societies where children occupy a position of low status, and corroborate the findings of other researchers (Somerset 1987; CHET-NA 1990; Knight et al. 1991).

Another factor, which the study identified as important if children are to be effective health educators, was the readiness of the school to raise the status of children and to enhance their credibility as educators in the eyes of their parents. A stronger link was found to be needed between the school and the community through the PTA to support teachers and parents in their efforts to develop a dialogue about health with children. It was found to be essential that the head teacher exercised strong leadership and supported the CHILD-to-child co-ordinator in the school.

Influences, problems and constraints One set of concerns centres around the financial security of the programme and the functioning of the management team: '[Identifying] more dependable sources of income must become a top priority for the Child-to-Child management team' (Somerset 1987: 104). This need is reiterated in the more recent evaluation (Babugura et al. 1993). UNICEF has provided financial support over many years, but no government funding has yet been made available to the programme. This is a problem that continues to resist solution.

Another set of concerns centres around the failure of the CHILD-to-child concept in Botswana to grow and evolve in response to the changes taking place in the concept around the world. By 1996 it had been recognized by stakeholders in the Ministries of Education, Health and Local Government and Lands, and by UNICEF, that the programme had become 'fatigued'. The numbers of schools recruited continued to rise but the overall level of activity within schools was decreasing. Strategies to revitalize the programme have since included reorganization of the management structure and recruitment of key people onto the management committee. The CHILD-to-child Foundation has been renamed the CHILD-to-child Network. The programme co-ordinator has remained in post since 1979. There has recently been a move supported by UNICEF to increase the participation of schools located in isolated settlements in the programme (Masolotate 1997). The following case study of CHILD-to-child in a settlement school identifies the lessons learned for future development of this programme as it expands in this direction.

CHILD-to-Child with Basarwa (Bushmen) Children in Botswana

As mentioned in the previous case study, there has recently been a move to increase the participation of settlement schools in the CHILD-to-child Little Teacher Programme in Botswana. In these schools the majority of children are Basarwa (Bushmen)[1] and 20 schools in remote settlements were scheduled to join the programme in 1998 (Masolotate 1997). It is therefore timely that this case study should analyse the experience of the CHILD-to-child Little Teacher Programme in a settlement school to draw out the lessons learned for future development of this programme. The case study demonstrates the influence of culture on children's learning in this school and examines how the Basarwa culture is being eroded through interaction with the formal education system. It argues for a more relevant bilingual, multicultural educational model through which the Child-to-Child approach could make an important contribution towards greater cultural equity and self-determination for the Basarwa.

The Basarwa are a minority population in Botswana. They are Bushmen who are ethnically interrelated and speak a collection of 'click' languages called Sesarwa. Serious questions have recently been raised concerning their rights: although they are generally recognized as the indigenous peoples of Botswana, they lack legal rights to land ownership and access to water sources. They have been subjected to prolonged marginalization and subjugation by the majority population of Tswana and other related Bantu tribes known as Batswana, who speak the national language called Setswana. Subjugation is recognized as a major barrier to Basarwa development and it underpins their increasing impoverishment (Mogwe 1992).

The Botswana government uses the name remote area dwellers (RADs) to group Basarwa together with the few Batswana who share their poor economic situation and location but are culturally distinct. This has been seen as a political strategy to acculturate the Basarwa and assimilate them into Batswana society (Saugestad 1993). Until recently the Basarwa have been politically silent but the recent growth of an 'indigenous' movement within Botswana is beginning to impact on the direction of social and political change by increasing the capacity of the Basarwa for self-determination. Saugestad (1993: 41) argues cogently that once indigenous organizations have been established and their leaders are able to negotiate with the government, far from threatening national unity and political stability, these organizations will contribute to the democratic process and actually make policy formulation and implementation easier.

Traditional patterns of learning and teaching in Basarwa society
Children learn within the family unit and the playgroup by watching
and 'doing' (Silberbauer 1981; Barnard 1993). The playgroup consists
of children from about three to six years, and much of their play is
imitation of the elders' daily activity. The knowledge, training and
socialization of the child in the playgroup thereby reinforce that
received from parents in the household. The egalitarian nature of
Basarwa society fosters co-operation rather than competition between
the sexes and age groups, and children do not play team games in
which in which an individual or group wins. High value is accorded
to harmony and complementarity within the band, and informal
singing and dancing make an important contribution to their social
and spiritual well-being (Marshall 1976; Barnard 1993).

Parental authority is kindly, neither parent is especially dominant
and children are allowed great freedom (see Silberbauer 1981). Children learn to respect and obey their parents and punishment of
children for disobedience is considered to be inappropriate and
unacceptable. Older siblings care for and teach younger siblings and
same-sex siblings enjoy a close relationship of trust and affection.
Girls learn many of their roles from their mothers, and consequently
spend more time with them than do boys. Brothers develop more
emotional independence in the playgroup because fathers are often
absent on hunting (or other) trips and children are not expected to
take any serious responsibility for hunting or gathering before their
mid-teens.

Researchers have noted a gradual breakdown of traditional Basarwa social organization indicative of the gradual assimilation of
Basarwa into the patriarchal Batswana society. Barnard (1993) reports
that when seasonal migration ceases children travel further from their
homes, adults spend less time with their children and women tend to
stay at home more while men are more likely to stay away from
home. Mogalakwe (1986) found that Ghanzi farmers increasingly used
child labour on the cattle-posts.

Schooling The government introduced free primary and secondary
education in 1988 and there are now primary day-schools in some of
the Ghanzi settlements, but there is a lack of boarding facilities.

Parents have difficulty caring for their children at the settlement schools because the land is not able to support the size of the resident population unless they make the unwelcome transition to subsistence farming. Parents therefore rely on being mobile in order to subsist, but many fear their children might be beaten or neglected if left with relatives (Lee 1984). Consequently Basarwa children still lack effective access to schooling, and this is reflected in low recruitment rates and high drop-out rates in settlement schools.

Lack of parental trust in schooling is a major barrier to enrolment. Parents believe schooling is breaking down their social traditions. They fear the occurrence of teenage pregnancies at the schools and believe Batswana men take advantage of their daughters because they do not respect Basarwa people. Children drop out of school because corporal punishment is used. According to Mogwe (1992) children are often punished because they cannot speak Setswana, the language of instruction.

A field study of the Little Teacher Programme in a settlement school
In 1992 an evaluation was undertaken to assess the effectiveness of little teachers in passing health messages to preschoolers and to their parents (Pridmore 1996). By extending the study to include a settlement school situated in Ghanzi District, western Botswana, it was possible to explore the influence of culture on the ability of little teachers to communicate health messages. In this school all the government schoolteachers were Batswana, and the social and economic disparity between them and the Basarwa living in the settlement was reflected in different standards of clothing and housing between children and teachers.

At the time of the study in 1992, 91 children were registered in the school and there were twelve preschool children attending for the Little Teacher Programme. The school population was highly mobile and most children were staying with relatives during term time and using government transport to travel between school and home for the vacations. There was a dramatic reduction in enrolment for the higher standards, especially for boys, indicating that girls were achieving greater access to schooling. This endorsed the findings of other researchers (Campbell, Main & Associates 1991).

The intervention　The teacher responsible for the Little Teacher Programme in the school taught four new health topics to the little teachers and supervised them while they passed on these messages to the preschool children using activity-based teaching methods. The preschool children were tested before and after the intervention to assess learning, and the little teachers were tested before and after they taught the preschool children to assess how much they learned from performing their role as little teachers. The teaching and testing were conducted in the official medium of instruction, Setswana. None of the teachers could speak Sesarwa, the children's mother tongue.

The knowledge test data were very difficult to interpret and we have to bear in mind that there were language, cultural and social barriers between the children and their teachers. In this context neither little teachers nor preschool children were able to learn the health messages taught during the intervention. In contrast, little teachers in the rural Batswana schools involved in the broader research study were able significantly to improve the learning of health messages by preschool children. Performing the role of a health educator also significantly increased the little teachers' own ability to recall health messages. These findings confirm that children learn better when they share the language, culture and social situation of their teachers.

Discussion: the need for a new educational model　The experience gained in the settlement school highlighted the way in which Basarwa children were multiply disadvantaged, and demonstrated the need for a more relevant model of schooling. The serious language barrier was exacerbated by a Western model of education relying on language as the main vehicle for learning, and was a major cause of the CHILD-to-child intervention programme failing to result in any measurable increase in learning. This corroborates the findings of other researchers (Kann 1989; Mogwe 1992) and highlights the importance of translation at all levels.

Social and cultural barriers to learning were also identified. Children cannot learn well if they are cold, hungry and not adequately cared for, or if what they are taught bears little resemblance to their own worldview. The cultural gap between schoolteachers and children prevented the teachers from playing their central role as a 'cultural bridge' to facilitate learning. It is significant that government policy does not acknowledge the distinct culture of Basarwa children at a time when educationists are increasingly aware that what matters most in the learning situation is the relationship between the culture of the learner (or group of learners) and the teacher (or the school). The traditional Western model of education in the school contrasted sharply with the traditional Basarwa model of learning and teaching where childhood learning in the family unit or playgroup was informal, non-competitive, task-orientated and relatively free of rules. Children learned through experience and experimentation or directly from elders. To increase the effectiveness of the curriculum educators at all levels would need to be open and willing to gain an intimate knowledge of Basarwa culture and able to use this knowledge to increase relevance and learning. This points to the need to recruit and train Basarwa teachers rapidly.

The experience confirmed that schooling is essentially a process of acculturation, a fact that is well recognized by educationists. Ideas and models of education imposed by those outside the culture of the child can prejudice the culture that the child brings into the learning situation. This experience is suggestive of the need for a new bilingual, multicultural educational model to overcome the barriers to access and to learning of Basarwa children. This model needs to seek a balance and consensus between Basarwa, Batswana and Western learning styles to enable Basarwa children to move into the wider society without sacrificing their own cultural identity. This would involve using more relevant 'indigenous' pedagogy (in which watching and doing are the main vehicles for learning), and adapting the present content so that it draws from experiences that are largely familiar and emphasize the culture of family and community. There are also indications of the need for improved teacher training. Traditional teacher training tends to select young people and take them away from their communities for training. This runs the risk of alienating them culturally and encouraging them to devalue their own culture. It may be more appropriate to select older Basarwa men and women who already provide a relevant informal pedagogy to children in the playgroup and train them within their community. This strategy has been used successfully in Primary Health Care Programmes to train traditional birth attendants as community health workers.

The potential of Child-to-Child The experience in the settlement school highlighted problems with the Little Teacher Programme. There is, however, considerable potential for the Child-to-Child approach to promote the learning of Basarwa children if it can be sensitively adapted to the context. Child-to-Child advocates the use of active learning methods (song, dance, games and stories) which are already part of traditional Basarwa pedagogy and could be used to increase relevance and reaffirm their knowledge systems and social organization. Child-to-Child could help children to think critically about their health problems, improve their self-image and self-esteem, develop leadership skills and enable children to have a voice within their family and community. Older children could help younger siblings to learn Setswana and so ease their entry into government schools. Basarwa children would be in a good position to pass health messages to their families and communities because of the egalitarian nature of their society, and Child-to-Child could be used to build a bridge between home and school. Children and parents/guardians could become empowered to develop this new model of education through consultation.

It is to be hoped that the Basarwa will eventually gain a political voice and negotiate a more self-determined model of education. The continued growth of the indigenous movement and the use of innovative educational approaches like Child-to-Child can play an important role. Ultimately, however, the development of the indigenous movement will revolve around the issue of whose culture matters and whose pedagogy matters. This is a political debate, and the Basarwa will need to develop the ability to speak with one voice and to make that voice heard.

Summary This case study highlights the inadequacy of the current model of schooling delivered to Basarwa children in Botswana and contends that their education should be re-evaluated from a cultural viewpoint. Children and teachers are embedded in a dynamic, cultural, social and political web, and serious language and cultural barriers to learning exist. These barriers underscore the need for a bilingual, multicultural model of education to affirm and strengthen the culture of the child. The high mobility of the Basarwa demands a flexible, less formal model of schooling and training of teachers from within the Basarwa culture. An innovative curriculum is needed, building on the traditional Basarwa pedagogy and worldview to develop skills needed to gain greater equity. The approach to health education known as Child-to-Child has considerable potential for curriculum development. Until a more relevant educational model is available Basarwa children will continue to be disadvantaged. It is to be hoped that in extending the Little Teacher Programme into more settlement schools adequate care and attention will be given to contextualizing the curriculum.

The Child-to-Child Co-ordinating Unit in Uganda

In 1994 the government of Uganda initiated a countrywide situational analysis to access any changes in the situation of women and children since the previous analysis in 1989. Six 'leading social and physical well-being problems' were identified (Republic of Uganda/UNICEF 1994), which provide some indication of the contextual landscape in which Child-to-Child activities occur.

Basic indicators of national health and well-being   Life expectancy, mortality rates, population growth rate, literacy levels, the prevalence of AIDS, and the provision of safe water and sanitation are key determinants of health and well-being (see Table 7.1). These figures confirm that there are high levels of mortality and of population growth, despite the toll being taken by the AIDS epidemic. Literacy rates and access to water and sanitation are low.

The Child-to-Child co-ordinating unit operates out of the Institute of Teacher Education at Kyambogo (ITEK) on the outskirts of the capital, Kampala. As we shall see when discussing its development, an emphasis has been placed on co-ordinating a network of geographical clusters or zones of Child-to-Child schools.

Getting started   The ITEK co-ordination unit was established in

Table 7.1 Vital statistics for Uganda

Life expectancy*	44 years
Infant mortality*	111 per 1,000 live births
Under-five mortality*	185 per 1,000 live births
Maternal mortality*	1,200 per 100,000 live births
Population growth rate**	2.5% per year
AIDS: total cases reported by 1993**	43,875
AIDS: cases per million**	2,314
Orphans (one or both parents dead)**	1.2 million (11.3%)
Adult literacy*	62%
Female literacy (as % of males) (1995)*	68%
Access to safe water*	38%
Access to adequate sanitation*	64%

Sources: * UNICEF 1998; ** Republic of Uganda/UNICEF 1994.

collaboration with UNICEF in 1983. In 1987 the unit moved to its present location at Kyambogo, the foremost teacher training college in Uganda, and soon established itself as an effective, albeit small (two or three full-time workers) unit. The focus of Child-to-Child activities was to be decentralized via a zonal system. In November 1994 there were between 7 and 270 schools in the 21 zones and within each participating school a school health club managed largely by the children themselves. As with Child-to-Child activities in other countries, the support of UNICEF was crucial, although Uganda has also benefited from support from Comic Relief, AMREF, Redd Barna and Voluntary Service Overseas (which posted a full-time volunteer to the ITEK for two years from 1994 to 1996). This financial support was accompanied by support from leading Ugandan educators such as Professor Sentaza Kujubi, formerly vice-chancellor of Makerere University.

Development of the programme By 1994 the zonal system had developed to the extent that it was estimated that there were approximately seven hundred schools, five teachers' colleges and over fifty pre-schools involved in some form of Child-to-Child activity. One hundred and ten of these schools are assumed to be 'active', with thirty-two described by the zonal co-ordinators as 'model schools'.

ITEK has three priorities:

1. to develop an activity-based health curriculum in the training of teacher tutors;
2. to work with government and non-government agencies in Uganda with the aim of transforming passive, classroom-based learning about health to learning that is linked to the immediate improvement of health in the school and surrounding community; and
3. to strengthen links between the health and education sectors at all levels.

The second priority area, which is classroom-focused, has been promoted in a number of significant ways: a large number of training workshops have been held to sensitize teachers to more active learning methodologies, Child-to-Child committees have been set up in many schools to oversee implementation of various activities, and a number of 'twinning schemes' have been initiated in which a younger child selects an older 'friend' or 'twin' to act as a mentor in the acquisition of new health knowledge and behaviour.

Other developments include:

- Training: in 1995, the unit organized five 'awareness' workshops to introduce Child-to-Child approaches to parents, teachers and students new to the approach.
- Material production: a newsletter is produced annually and a 30-minute radio broadcast goes out each week on radio Uganda.
- Teacher training: students taking courses at ITEK are now able to follow a Child-to-Child programme integrated into their pre-sessional teacher education course.
- Research: ITEK is home to an internationally funded research project, which has recently concluded its work and is reported on in the next section.
- Networking: the co-ordinating unit works with a number of other NGOs including AIDS Relief Uganda, ANPCCAN (African Network for the Prevention and Protection against Child Abuse and Neglect) and the Ugandan Paediatrics Association.

Influences, problems, constraints: findings from research In 1993 funds were secured by the Child-to-Child Trust in London to investigate the impact of a one-year Child-to-Child programme in a selected cluster of Ugandan schools. With the specific aim of assessing the effect of Child-to-Child approaches to health education upon the knowledge, self-concept, behaviour, attendance and academic performance of children within the chosen schools, the research produced findings of interest to those seeking evidence of the efficacy of such an approach to health education in Uganda and more generally elsewhere.

Two hundred and forty seven children in 17 schools in and around Kampala took part in a controlled study, which found that at the end of the year the study group of children (those in schools where Child-to-Child had been introduced) scored significantly higher in self-concept-rated behaviour in school and a rating of their positive behaviour towards other children. The study group children had significantly fewer days' absence from school. Significantly, the research also found no differences in academic attainment or in health knowledge between the two groups.

In terms of school processes, in the study group the social and educational behaviour of the children improved, with teachers reporting positively on the motivation of children and on their own teaching. However, a great deal needs to be done in improving the methodology, providing better resourcing of classrooms and reducing the backwash effect of examinations on the curriculum. The qualitative data also found little direct evidence of a favourable impact upon academic achievement or in health knowledge.

This research has implications for the development of Child-to-Child in Uganda, and possibly elsewhere, in four major areas: on the teaching and learning process in school; on the children and teachers involved; on the management of such innovations at national and school level, and on the search for solutions to problems identified by the research. Generally speaking Child-to-Child appears to improve the quality of the teaching and learning process. The 'twinning' of older and younger pupils and the establishment of family 'clubs' throughout the school fits well into a society structured around communal and hierarchical value systems.

Schools in Uganda spend a lot of time studying topics related to personal and environmental health, immunization and AIDS, areas that mirror the 1994 situational analysis referred to earlier. Other areas that appear to be more difficult to teach, such as poverty, malnutrition and the 'lack of voice for women', were largely absent in the schools researched. The focus on environmental health is having some impact on improving the environs of the school (e.g. buckets of water near the latrines, waste-bins clearly marked), but sometimes seems to degenerate into activities where children are just sweeping the compound with little learning in evidence.

Although the relationship between teacher and pupil in all the Child-to-Child schools improved (with many teachers reporting working 'with' rather than 'against' the children) there was, regrettably, no enhanced academic performance in the areas of mathematics, English and science. Some evidence exists, however, to suggest that a more collaborative teaching style in the experimental schools is helping improve pupils' vocabulary acquisition, reading and mathematics work and is improving the children's research skills.

The impact of the Child-to-Child approach on teachers and pupils was more significant. At the end of the school year, study group children scored significantly higher in the self-concept-rated behaviour in school and a rating of their positive behaviour towards other children. As with performance in English, mathematics and science, there were no significant differences between the two groups of children in acquisition of health knowledge. Children in the Child-to-Child schools enjoyed the way they learned, with children showing a more focused and realistic view of what they could achieve. Teachers in the study schools reported a more broadened repertoire of teaching styles although the practice seemed patchy, with teachers concerned at the amount of preparation required and the possible detrimental effect it might have on 'covering the syllabus'. The most successful schools were those in which the head teacher fully involved him- or herself in the approach.

Management of Child-to-Child programmes in Uganda is de-centralized and so the roles of head teachers and the community leaders are more important in the sustainability of the programmes. Head teachers often saw Child-to-Child as an approach promoting good pupil discipline and an improved school 'image' rather than an essentially educational endeavour aiming to improve more funda-mental aspects of teaching and learning. There is a case to be made for communicating the ideas behind Child-to-Child more effectively to those in positions of responsibility.

Teachers and pupils identified problems in adopting new approaches to health education: low teacher motivation, the predominance of examinations and a lack of resources to sustain more child-centred work. Certain topics, such as 'water' and 'hygiene', were perceived as easy to teach, with others requiring more specialized knowledge – tuberculosis, for instance, was viewed as problematic. Solutions provided by teacher and pupils ranged from in-service courses in school to the production of 'home-grown' learning materials to the building up of school resource centres. What is noticeable is the value attached to solving problems at the school, in the school, a consequence no doubt of the priority given to the decentralization of Child-to-Child activities in Uganda.

Developing Local Child-to-Child Resource Units: the Ghana Experience

A major current priority of the Child-to-Child Trust is the encouragement of local resource units and networks that can more readily, and more appropriately, meet local needs and challenges. In Ghana the Child-to-Child Network was recently established, bringing together two major initiatives based at the University College of Education at Winneba (UCEW) and the Afram Plains (Childscope). Winneba, a coastal fishing community to the east of Cape Coast, is the centre of the newly established University College of Education, a constituent tertiary institution of the University of Cape Coast established to provide teacher education training at the basic education level for Ghana's teacher training colleges and primary and junior secondary schools.

The Institute of Education, Development and Extension (IEDE) was established at the University College in the early 1990s to, among other things, devise and implement innovative schemes to raise the quality of pre- and in-service education for teachers: programmes by distance education, the promotion of action research in local schools, and the development of Child-to-Child school-based programmes.

The Afram Plains District in Ghana's Eastern Province is one of the poorer areas of the country detrimentally affected by the Aka-sombo Dam in the early days of independence.

UNICEF Ghana, through a local NGO (PRONET), organizes a school improvement programme called 'Childscope'. One of its components is a higher education project using the Child-to-Child approach, which includes both local training and monitoring. Initially (1995–96) six schools were involved, but there are plans gradually to increase the number of schools included.

Getting started At Winneba the IEDE unit began small. An aware-ness-raising workshop, funded by UNICEF Ghana and the British ODA, brought together selected teachers and the head teachers of five local primary schools. This workshop was facilitated by experienced health educators drawn from the Ghana Education Service and the University College of Education (along with representatives of the Afram Plains project). Five schools and upper primary classes were identified and class action plans drawn up, with regular monitoring planned by the unit based at the University College.

In the Afram Plains the project began in March 1995 with an aim to (i) improve primary education so children can read, write and be numerate by the end of primary school; (ii) maintain (or increase) enrolment; and (iii) increase attendance and continuation rates, especially of girls. Whereas the Winneba activities concentrated on the teacher–child relationship and the production of child-centred, community-focused classroom work, the Afram Plains initiative took as its focus from the beginning the role communities can play in improving their schools, as well as helping them develop realistic approaches to addressing the issues their schools encounter.

Development of the programme The Winneba project has developed to include four more schools. A follow-up workshop was held at the University College in January 1995 involving all teachers in all the schools. The problem of successful implementation was addressed with 'mini-workshops' planned for the participating schools, with thought given to the issue of where in the curriculum Child-to-Child should be taught. With the Ghana Ministry of Education reviewing its life skills syllabus, Winneba Child-to-Child activists considered the role that 'carrier' subjects such as English, maths and science can play in establishing health education within the school.

The community-focused work within the Afram Plains took a different route. Participatory Rural Appraisal (PRA) has been carried out in four sets of communities surrounding the five sub-district schools identified in the project. The goals of the PRA were: (i) to determine the level of interaction between the school and community and how the relationship between the two affects the quality of schooling; (ii) to encourage the communities to take initiatives in identifying school problems and developing creative yet realistic solutions; and (iii) to facilitate greater interaction between schools and communities to address issues in and around the school.

The PRA exercise, lasting 13 days, proved to be an effective tool in generating community interest and participation in identifying, analysing and acting upon issues regarding the local school, and also provided the team with lessons learned.

As already mentioned, recent development has been the establishment of a Ghana Child-to-Child Network, which grew out of a meeting of Ghanaian health educators (notably from Winneba and the Afram Plains), at a Child-to-Child short course, 'Planning Health Promotion in Schools', in London in 1995. Members of the network include the Childscope team in the Afram Plains, representatives of the Ministry of Education in Accra, the School Health Action Plan (SHAP), UNICEF (through PRONET) and co-ordinated from Winneba by the network co-ordinator, Mr Paul Ackom. Essentially the network aims to replicate many of the activities carried out by the Trust in London but at a national level, focusing in particular on the sharing of ideas and experiences, and the carrying of the Child-to-Child approach to other areas of the country. Funding for the network was initially provided by UNICEF. Recently members of the network team have carried out development work within a very poor area of Accra, Nima, working with a cluster of schools sharing a large urban campus, developing similar activities to those in Winneba. Funding for this has come from the charity Bread for the World. The work has now been evaluated, with attention paid not only to what has been achieved but also to lessons that have been learned.

Influences, problems, constraints: lessons learned Given the relatively small number of activists within the IEDE unit at Winneba, a great deal has been achieved during the past four years: a cluster of nine schools have now implemented school action plans, the success of these depending to a large extent upon the leadership provided in-school by the head teachers and the encouragement and monitoring provided by the Institute of Education Development and Extension Unit's team.

Its success has been in the raising of awareness and the design of school-based programmes, but a major constraint concerns the sustainability of the programme within the schools. The Ghana primary education system is currently under review, with nationwide efforts to establish 'free, compulsory, universal, basic education' (FCUBE). School syllabuses are to be slimmed down, head teachers retrained, the examination system reformed to include more continuous assessment, and management decentralized to the districts. All this has produced a situation where initiatives, planning and change have taken precedence over implementation, continuity and sustainability. An interesting development at Winneba has been the collaboration of the Child-to-Child and Action Research Units, with the latter strengthening the work of the former. The extension of the Winneba team's work to include the management of a Child-to-Child development project within the Nima area of Accra, a two-hour road journey away, raises a number of questions concerning the 'engine' of growth of local resource centres. Whether the network at Winneba will be able to provide 'fuel' for its own development plans will depend on maintenance of the energy and commitment provided by its core members, funding, particularly from within the country, and the success of the ministerial efforts to decentralize educational development.

The Afram Plains team is also in a position to identify lessons in the planning, implementation and networking of their activities. UNICEF (1996) has noted in its *Childscope Monitoring and Process Report* that in planning the PRA exercise, 'sufficient time must be allocated for training team members, both in PRA methodology and facilitation in general'. In implementing PRAs the team found that the following five issues underlay the extent and effectiveness of the communities' involvement:

1. Parents believe that education is important, but, because they do not see the direct benefits, they do not have a proactive attitude towards their children's schooling.
2. Initially, community members viewed their schools as separate entities from the community, which belonged to the government.
3. There are no functioning community-based school management bodies such as PTAs.
4. School–community relationships are more positive when the teachers live in the community where the school is located.
5. The time and energy children spend on the household responsibilities given to them are especially significant for girls, who are given responsible for the majority of household chores such as fetching water and preparing food.

In looking to the workshop as a means of disseminating Child-to-Child activities it became clear that the participants need to be made aware from the beginning that a major expectation is that they will go back and train their colleagues, and that they should be given support to do so. However, the problem of teachers incorporating new ideas learned at workshops into their classroom teaching is also identified as a major challenge. These lessons, which apply to some extent to the Winneba work, need to be viewed in the light of the fundamental process-orientated philosophy that underpins the activities of the Ghana network. If Child-to-Child is to succeed it will do so locally, with teams of enthusiasts joining forces to support common endeavours and approaches. It will also need to recognize the flexibility required for every school, community and district to capitalize on its unique qualities.

Note

1. The name 'Bushmen' is now being positively embraced by the Basarwa, because they feel that it most accurately reflects their origins as hunters and gatherers and underscores their right to remain in their traditional hunting lands.

IV

Reaching Children for Health

8

Lessons Learned and Implications for Research, Policy and Practice

In this book we have argued that there is a need to examine innovative approaches to health education such as Child-to-Child in order to increase our understanding of how the ideas and methods are being practised in different contexts and to learn how to strengthen the approach. In the final chapter we summarize the arguments put forward in the book, draw out the lessons learned for policy and make recommendations for future action and research.

Critical Analysis of the Child-to-Child Approach to Health Education

This analysis has shown that Child-to-Child was originally formulated as an international programme designed to teach and encourage schoolchildren to concern themselves with the health, welfare and development of their younger brothers and sisters and of other children younger than themselves in the community. This formulation has broadened over time to affirm the power of children to influence their own age group, their families and their communities. However, the underlying philosophy continues to maintain a deep commitment to the three original principles: Primary Health Care, children as agents of change, partnerships for health.

Child-to-Child is promoted as an innovative approach, which respects but at the same time challenges traditional models of health education. This approach builds on the tradition of children helping each other and their families and sharing their ideas, but rejects the low position traditionally occupied by children in the social hierarchy.

We have argued that this balancing of respect for tradition with commitment for change is in reality a sophisticated approach more easily understood in theory than applied in the field, where the risk will always be that traditional assumptions about the role of the child will prevail.

Supporters of Child-to-Child claim that the approach is sufficiently flexible to be adapted to different cultural contexts and to be owned by those implementing it. We have argued that where Child-to-Child is adapted to the local context there is the risk of the essence of the approach being compromised or lost. Concern for children themselves, always fundamental to the philosophy of Child-to-Child, may not always have been evident in practice. Many programmes lack an understanding of the child-centred methodology promoted by Child-to-Child, which challenges children to think and to solve problems for themselves.

Child-to-Child advocates a particular methodology in health education, but it also presupposes a Western frame of mind about children and their status in society at variance with received attitudes of many non-Western cultures. Child-to-Child methods and materials will not of themselves win sought-for health changes where traditional assumptions about children still hold sway. We argue that it remains to be seen how far Child-to-Child can overcome traditional resistance to the principle of children as agents of change by those who do not share Western assumptions about children. We contend that changing minds will prove as formidable an obstacle to the implementation of Child-to-Child as changing the structural, economic and social conditions that impede its realization in practice. Consequently we have questioned the extent to which practice and theory have corresponded, and how far the approach has ever really been fully implemented. We have had to ask how far Child-to-Child remains 'a dream that has yet to come true'.

While recognizing that no one 'owns' Child-to-Child, the Trust has accepted that there must be some guidance, if not some control, as to how the movement's approach is to be interpreted and implemented. Child-to-Child as a series of related ideas and ideas can be altered beyond recognition. We have noted that Child-to-Child is practised in widely disparate ways, some of which are hardly recognizable as

Child-to-Child and which, for all our difficulty in defining the character of Child-to-Child, reflect neither the principles nor the methodology of its approach as most would understand them.

The lack of control exerted over implementation of Child-to-Child contrasts strikingly with the firm control exerted over some other educational approaches, which have 'top-down' rather than 'bottom-up' structures. For example, in the 'Reading Recovery' Scheme developed in New Zealand by Marie Clay, very firm control is retained over its curriculum, its training mechanisms and its 'quality' (Clay and Watson 1982).

The possibility of introducing some form of 'vetting' of initiatives claiming to use Child-to-Child has been raised, but notions of control are not easily compatible with the ethos of Child-to-Child. The Trust has always made a point of setting aside ownership of ideas, pro-grammes, projects and materials and has encouraged people to adapt the ideas to their own context. Consequently accreditation is not yet being seriously considered. However, the Trust is currently interested in developing clusters of resource persons, regionally or nationally, who would play an important role in reducing the gap between theory and practice.

A major plank of Child-to-Child's work in London is the produc-tion of teaching–learning materials to support the curriculum. As we saw in Chapter 5 this activity has developed considerably, with the Trust not only producing materials in a number of first languages but also supplementary readers, newsletters, and a broad range of resource materials for the health educator working through the educa-tion system. A critical review of the use of these publications in three national contexts reveals concerns about Child-to-Child that go beyond the production of teaching–learning materials – for example, the fact that the materials are essentially aimed at the teacher and require training for the teacher to use them in a child-centred way, the problematic absence of ways to assess a child's learning and the limited amount of locally produced materials.

The Trust's commitment to the support of local resources centres and networks (for example in Bangladore with the South India Re-source Group) is a welcome development and has implications for the encouragement of locally driven research.

Lessons Learned from the Case Studies

The first case study, from Nepal, provides lessons of a fundamental nature concerning the promotion of a developmental model – in two phases. In this model children are first encouraged to take up a modest role as the carriers of health messages to their community and then, when they and their elders feel happy with their new role, they are encouraged to play a much more decisive role and one that is currently occupied by their parents and teachers. The question of the agency of child or children in promoting and carrying through change lies at the heart of what is attractive and at the same time problematic about child-empowering development.

A notable feature of the Child-to-Child work in Oaxaca, Mexico, is its community focus and its strong sense of local ownership – for example, in the development and production of learning materials. The Mexico case study also reveals the problem of being able to select and then provide adequate and long-term support for the 'guides' or teachers, particularly given the reliance upon the help of volunteers.

The development of Child-to-Child in the United Kingdom, as shown in the Merseyside case study, illustrates the thorny problem of the location of health education within the curriculum, particularly in a system that is centrally controlled and gives increasing priority to the learning of the core subjects of English, maths and science. A way forward attempted in Merseyside, and at Winneba in Ghana too, is to stress the cross-curricular role Child-to-Child can play in enhancing core subjects, particularly in the development of skills and attitudes. Such an orientation means, however, that Child-to-Child has to be viewed as something more than just the delivery of narrowly conceived health education content.

The Little Teacher Programme in Botswana illustrates challenges of financial sustainability and community impact. Without government funds such a programme has an uncertain future and, perhaps more importantly, makes integration of innovation within the mainstream education system much harder to achieve. The effectiveness of the programme in terms of community impact and involvement appears mixed, with evaluation (Pridmore 1996) showing a positive increase in the number of health messages passed from girls to female relatives within the home, but parents indicating that they have little time or opportunity to communicate with their offspring. It is recognized that this programme could usefully be broadened so that the needs of the older children (the Little Teachers) could be taken more fully into account. The hardest question is how far it is fair to expect in societies such as rural Botswana the kind of thinking and rethinking that the development of Child-to-Child demands. If this criticism is fair it is less an adverse reflection on the culture of Botswana than a comment on the academic culture in which the philosophy of Child-to-Child originated and where its ideas continue to be debated with greater facility.

The case study of CHILD-to-child with Basarwa (Bushmen) children in a settlement school in Botswana illustrates how young children can be educationally compromised because they do not know Setswana, the language of instruction in the school, and because there are cultural and social barriers to their learning. The lesson learned here is that we need more effective and appropriate models of educational provision. For the Basarwa children the model needs to be both intercultural and bilingual.

The major lessons to be learned from the Uganda case study concern the nature of children's learning. On the positive side, the research conducted among schoolchildren in Kampala indicated that Child-to-Child is successful in developing their self-concept, their behaviour towards each other, and their motivation for learning about health issues. The paucity of evidence showing any positive impact upon academic attainment level or level of health knowledge is more worrying and requires further research. The problems teachers face in adjusting their methodology and in sustaining more child-centred creative work within an examinations-dominated curriculum are echoed in many of the case studies.

Getting Child-to-Child ideas from well-attended and popular teacher workshops into the day-to-day life of the classroom is a major challenge worldwide. In the two sites featured in the Ghanaian case study this issue and the problem of sustaining the teacher *in situ* raise fundamental questions about the most effective way Child-to-Child implements its ideas. Up to now the 'workshop' has been a favoured method (particularly in Ghana) for the dissemination of new ideas, but there is some evidence to suggest that methods that locate the teacher within the classroom, e.g. team teaching, and the involvement of in-service support via head teacher training (Hawes and Stephens 1990), may be more economical and more effective.

Implications of the Review

For health education This book has highlighted the importance of local adaptation of health education initiatives being informed by a detailed and sensitive understanding of the social, cultural and environmental contexts within which programmes are being implemented. The need for such information has been widely advocated (see Mullen and Zapaka 1989; Francis 1993; Van der Vynckt 1992/3) and noted in the introduction. Much useful information has also been provided that could be used to support an educational and environmental approach to health promotion planning. Such information is necessary to support the application of robust planning frameworks such as the PRECEDE-PROCEED framework developed by Green and Kreuter (1991). We have argued that robust planning frameworks should be used to increase the relevance and effectiveness of health education provided that they adopt a participatory approach to working with communities from the very outset of the planning process.

This review has also contributed to our knowledge of the way in which sophisticated concepts can be misunderstood and misinterpreted in their implementation. Concepts such as the right of the child to participate as a partner in health have been developed in relation to the so-called 'global' child. We would argue that such a child exists only in theory. In reality there are many different children and many different childhoods. Moreover, there is little agreement among those who advocate child participation about what this really means. The notion that children have a right to participate is a difficult concept in many societies where age and gender are important aspects of social hierarchies. We have seen that in moving from the 'global' child, a notional entity, to the 'local' child, the empirical child born in one place and at one time, the essence of important ideas about the nature of partnership with children can be lost. This gulf between the ideal and the actual is not surprising in communities where equitable partnership between adults (let alone between children and adults) is not part of the social structure. We contend that in some societies the concept of partnership with children is so new that it is virtually impossible for people to grasp it. However, even if we must accept that the process of achieving partnership with children may take many generations, it remains a necessary goal. In this respect Child-to-Child serves as a compass for health education. The destination may be distant but Child-to-Child has shown the direction clearly.

The review presented in this book lends support for the model of learning put forward by Little (1992). We saw in Chapter 2 that, according to this model, learning occurs only if the gap between what the learner and the teacher each bring to the so-called 'learning arena' is capable of being bridged. This gap results from a combination of differences in knowledge, learning methods, reasons for learning and outcomes of learning. In one of the Botswana case studies the inability of Basarwa children to learn the health messages in the context of the settlement school suggests that for these children the gap was too wide to be breached. This failure to bridge the gap is important not only because the children did not learn the health messages but also because, according to Little's model, the failure could hinder future learning.

For the conceptualization of Child-to-Child The case studies revealed a range of interpretations of the character and purpose of Child-to-Child. We have to ask whether Child-to-Child, in terms of 'the right of children to participate fully in establishing a healthy and meaningful life for themselves and for others', does not lend itself to being 'diluted' in cultures where the role of children is seen very differently from the way in which it is seen in the West. Where Child-to-Child challenges local attitudes about what children are allowed to participate in, the undertow of traditional assumptions will always be pulling against the direction in which Child-to-Child is seeking to move. The implications are that Child-to-Child must take greater account of the extent to which it has worked with this Western frame of mind, that it must recognize more seriously the degree to which non-Western societies will be resistant to aspects of its approach, and that it must investigate more fully how far its essential principles can be assimilated within such cultures. Only then could it be shown whether the 'Child-to-Child dream' can come true.

For the effectiveness of children as health educators The review has highlighted the way in which the acceptability of children as health educators within their family and community needs to be strengthened. The fundamental reason for the unwillingness to accept children as health educators is their low status within society. We have argued that this problem needs to be addressed within a larger debate on social organization and the rights of the child. The finding that most messages are passed from girls to their mothers (or other women) implies that Child-to-Child can be a useful means of educating women about health. This is an important implication because of the strong and well-established link between maternal education and the mortality rates of infants and young children noted in Chapter 2.

More generally we argue that the fundamental principles that underpin Child-to-Child (children's participation in the learning process, community-oriented education, greater relevance of the curriculum to the child's needs now and in the future, recognition of the role of the teacher as facilitator rather than 'lecturer' in the classroom, etc.) have implications for those wishing to effect changes in educational policy that move beyond the rhetorical. In Ghana and Nepal, for example, we can see Child-to-Child providing policy-makers with models of good practice that illustrate not only effective ways of delivering health education but new approaches, rooted in the world of the classroom and the village, to 'good' education applicable across the curriculum. The support of Child-to-Child by agencies such as UNICEF and the Save the Children Fund (UK) is indicative of the recognition that, as an approach to learning, Child-to-Child has potential to act as a model of educational change.

For educational policy change The Basawa case study from Botswana argues that current educational policy is increasing inequalities by undermining the effectiveness of schooling for the Basarwa. Children learn better when they share the language, culture and social situation of their teachers. Ideas and models of education imposed by those outside the culture of the child can prejudice the culture that the child brings into the learning situation. We have to question why the government is insisting on Setswana as the only medium of instruction in schools at a time when Sesarwa-speaking schoolteachers are not available to facilitate communication.

For curriculum reform Many writers have stressed that the curriculum must reflect an intimate understanding of the values and perceptions of the learners if it is to be seen to be relevant to them (Aikman 1994b; Carr-Hill 1994a; Leach 1994). All our case studies argue for a new educational model. Such a model would need to achieve a balance and consensus between indigenous language and learning styles and Western educational approaches in order to enable children like the Basarwa of Botswana to move into the wider society without sacrificing their own cultural identity. A more relevant 'indigenous' pedagogy needs to be developed that takes more account of a child's traditional upbringing and worldview. For many children the main vehicles for learning are watching and doing within the familiar world of family and community, the transition to school taking them away not only from what they know but also from the context within which they can act legitimately and effectively.

There are also implications for the training of teachers. Traditional teacher training tends to select young people and take them away from their communities for training, thus risking their becoming culturally alienated and encouraging them to view their own culture as disadvantageous to the role of schoolteacher. In many cultures it may be more appropriate to select as teachers more mature individuals who are not only respected for their position in society but who help children develop the skills needed to maintain a traditional way of life. This strategy has been successfully used in Primary Health Care programmes to train traditional birth attendants as community health workers.

Pridmore's research among the Basarwa of Botswana (Pridmore 1996) shows that if the ideas and methods can be sensitively adapted to the local context Child-to-Child has considerable potential for enhancing the learning environment of Basarwa children. The Child-to-Child Network at Winneba in Ghana provides evidence too that the use of active learning methods (song, dance, games, stories) that are part of traditional Fante pedagogy have the potential to increase the relevance of the school curriculum and to reaffirm the children's own knowledge systems and social organization. The Child-to-Child methodology could also challenge children to think critically about their health problems as well as developing their self-sufficiency and leadership skills. Such children would then be in a good position to help their communities develop and move forward. In Basarwa society egalitarian values mean that children have great potential to become the engine of change and development. The Uganda case study also provides evidence of how Child-to-Child as an example of 'good' Western-style education enhances the community's view of the school and the role of the young learner in society.

Recommendations for Future Action and Research

At the international level A wider debate needs to be developed on the nature of children's participation in development. This debate is currently most active in relation to the rights of children in civil society (i.e. the domain in which a child is a citizen) (see IIED 1996) but it needs to be broadened to include their rights as partners in health. If children are to participate we also need to consider how their participation can be assessed and to develop new and more appropriate measures. A start has been made by Hart (1992, 1997) who, in developing his so-called 'Ladder of Participation' for children, borrowed the ladder metaphor from Arnstein's (1971) essay on adult participation. In Chapter 4 we argued that this is an emotive issue that clearly needs more careful and sensitive study.

A wider debate is also needed to examine what is central and non-negotiable to Child-to-Child and to address the major concerns about the approach that have been raised in this book. More case studies are needed to examine the extent to which Child-to-Child has been put into practice without its distinctive approach being compromised.

One way forward for Child-to-Child in the next millennium is to be found in the concept of the 'Healthy School' (WHO 1994, 1997). Here may be an opportunity for Child-to-Child to penetrate the formal education system, for so long resistant to change. This is an exciting possibility, enlisting as it would the support of just under a billion potential children as partners in health promotion. The potential for Child-to-Child to contribute further in this field is unlimited. Within the framework of WHO's Global School Health Initiative, Child-to-Child could provide a working model of how schools with their parents can set local social development priorities for health and how they can take account of these priorities in other core subjects such as maths, languages and science. By involving parents in what their children are doing, Child-to-Child could offer the possibility of a closer link between the school and community.

Educators need to be strongly challenged to accept the need for a 'whole school' approach to health, encouraging the teaching of health across the whole curriculum and aiming to make the health of the school a model for the community. Educators also need to be challenged to accept the need for a methodology that links learning with doing and schoolteaching to community needs and to health action. We need more examples of good practice in schools and we need to foster alliances between governmental and non-governmental groups at all levels to promote school health. A useful entry point for reform would be the development of 'new look' national health plans along the lines of those detailed by Bomba et al. (1994).

Developing a 'whole school' model is central to improving health through schooling and illustrates the breadth of the field into which Child-to-Child now needs to move. Child-to-Child involvement in 'healthy schools' programmes opens the way for developing a community curriculum, which recognizes the contribution children can make to achieve community goals. It also allows for the possibility of extending the use of the Child-to-Child methodology to other areas of experience beyond health, such as environmental and social studies, and the peer tutoring of subjects such as reading.

At the national level We need more well-designed research studies to evaluate the effectiveness of Child-to-Child and to understand the process better in different cultural contexts. One study is currently being developed by the authors of this book and involves investigation into the partnership between adults and children in different cultural contexts in relation to what is called comprehensive school health education. The research questions that guide this study are, we would suggest, exemplars of the type of research that needs to be carried out at national level:

- How are terms such as 'childhood', 'health' and 'partnership' understood internationally and in specific national contexts?
- What is the nature of the partnership between children and adults in the context of school and home?
- What factors promote and hinder the role of children and adults in the context of school and home?
- What strategies could be developed to increase the level of participation of children in the promotion of health?
- What are the implications of the research for policy-makers?

If 'what' is being asked is important then so is 'how', or the way in which research of this kind is carried out. The use of qualitative approaches to educational research in developing countries is now well known (Vulliamy et al. 1990), as is the use of action-oriented methods and those that promote the development of more culturally sensitive research approaches and techniques (Stephens 1998).

A final question concerns the dissemination and publication of locally generated research. It is beyond the scope of this book to discuss the issues concerning the domination by the 'North' of knowledge 'capital' generated in the 'South'. Suffice it to say that the Trust is in a good position with its support of local groups and networks to promote and facilitate indigenous research and publishing.

Action at the local level We have argued above for action that would use Child-to-Child as the entry point for launching innovative 'whole school' approaches to health. Many schools have already developed their own school health action plans (SHAP) along the lines of those currently being used in Kenya and elsewhere (Hawes 1992; Pridmore and Smith 1996). However, as we have emphasized, for children to be accepted as partners in health their status in many societies would have to change and such a change could only follow from a radical change of attitude towards them. Ultimately it is change at this level that is needed and that must remain the goal – however distant.

The various 'stakeholders' in the community – teachers, parents, guardians and health workers, not least children themselves – need to become involved in a process of participatory learning and action (PLA, see IIED 1995). The object of such a process must be to determine what the concept of Child-to-Child means within their situation, to identify the constraints to children's participation, and to seek ways of increasing their acceptability as partners in health. It would also be useful to involve children in focus group discussions to identify the types of health messages which they would find easier to pass to their parents and those they would find more difficult.

Summary

This concluding chapter has summarized the main issues raised by the critical review of Child-to-Child presented in this book and drawn out the implications of these findings. Recommendations have been made for future research and action.

This book makes a contribution to the literature at a time when innovative approaches in health education are being sought and when a small window of opportunity has opened for health education to prove itself. It has argued for further debate and action to reduce the gap between the theory and the practice of Child-to-Child. It has provided evidence from case studies from around the world to illustrate the valuable contribution children can make to promoting health. Children can have a very strong power of advocacy, but they are highly vulnerable. Few people have yet developed the special skills needed to work with them as partners in health. It is well recognized that children's lives can be changed by the actions of adults, but it is not so widely accepted that children can themselves transform the lives of adults. This is where the future challenge lies.

Appendix 1: Resources and How to Use Them[1]

- What is needed and where help may be sought
- How to convince people to invest their time in school health promotion
- Human resources at national and local level; how to use them
- Material Resources, especially written ones, and where to obtain them

If we are to introduce comprehensive health promotion into our schools we will need the resources to do it. Resources include:

Money

For most people the word resources means money. Comprehensive school health education will require money for training and for resource materials. The amounts needed are not great. If a country, a local project or a school wishes to start a reasonable programme it is likely that it will find support to do so. There is much concern about health in schools. Therefore, many international and national agencies and NGOs, and even private businesses and individuals may be prepared to help programmes get started. They need only to be convinced that such projects will be effective in improving the health of children and communities.

This is not to say that money will not be needed to meet some needs identified by the programme. In many cases the causes of poor health are closely linked to community needs such as poor water supply and sanitation, lack of land and food, environmental pollution

The following large agencies have supported programmes, which include new approaches to school health:

UNICEF
DfID (British Aid, formerly ODA)
Danida (Danish Aid)
Cida (Canadian Aid)
Save the Children Fund, UK
Rada Barnan (SCF Sweden)
AMREF (East Africa)
Comic Relief (Africa)
CRY (Child Relief and You), India
The Aga Khan Foundation
The Bernard Van Leer Foundation
PLAN International

together with a number of agencies and religious bodies. Often embassies from European or North American countries are able to make small grants without referring to their national aid agencies.

and poor housing, all of which require a great deal of money to put right. But lack of funds or poor health conditions should never prevent a programme from starting. There is always something that schools can do and one of the most important things is to get children and adults talking about their health needs and making them known clearly and loudly to those who may be able to help them.

Time

What is more difficult to find than money is time. Making schools and communities healthier takes time: time to plan, time to convince people, time to teach and learn new things.

In order for people to spend time they must really be convinced that the new ideas are worthwhile. This book is filled with ideas and experience, which, if used, can make comprehensive school health

Comprehensive school health promotion – some arguments worth using

- *50% of the world's population are children. We owe it to them to provide effective health education NOW.*
- *Healthy teachers find teaching easier and teach better. They act as an example to children and help to provide a positive go-ahead atmosphere in the school.*
- *Healthy children do better at school.*
- *Healthy schools (especially those where children learn life skills through health education) get better academic results.*
- *Currently many children enter school with disadvantages because their health has suffered as a result of conditions during pregnancy and during early childhood. We need to educate future mothers and fathers, where we can reach them – at SCHOOL.*
- *Children in school are frequently unhealthy and unhappy. This affects their learning as well as their being. Good health promotion in school can help these children especially during their adolescence, and save them from wasting their lives and their schools' time and effort.*
- *Comprehensive school health promotion teaches children to act responsibly in looking after their own health. We need this responsible thought and action more today than ever before.*
- *Working TOGETHER we can improve our health and the health of our communities and our environment.*
- *Health promotion is thus an investment in development.*

programmes both interesting and effective. Unless these ideas are spread among many people and *unless people are able to say these are our* ideas, *we* talked about them, *we* developed them, *we* explained them to others and *we* saw them working, *then they will never catch on.* Spreading the information about the programme, getting people to talk about it also takes time, but it is time very well spent.

Human Resources (People) at National Level

The table below suggests some of the people at national level who may be able to help when comprehensive school health-promotion programmes are being organized. It is drawn from experience in organizing health action programmes involving 'children for health'.

Politicians May be interested in the idea. *Better Health for our Schools*, and *Children for Health* are strong statements. But be careful. Politicians often want ideas to spread very quickly and reach out to all citizens, so explain that the movement must grow slowly.

Policy-makers and planners in health and education Potential organizers of programmes at national level are also necessary to provide support and 'blessing' for local programmes. Let us hope that they fully understand the concept of comprehensive school health promotion and that different sectors all have the same view and co-operate one with another.

University staff Always interested in new approaches and may agree to 'write up' the programme or to involve their students in describing or evaluating local activities in schools. University paediatricians may well co-operate in 'Training of trainers' courses.

Teachers' associations These often support school-based action and have proved interested in the idea of health-promoting schools. There is similar support from their international body, Education International.

Organizers of national voluntary bodies (NGOs) Scouts, Guides and other youth groups are always interested in health action programmes involving children. They fit in well with the 'badge system'. Other bodies which concentrate on specific areas of health such as clean water, hygiene and sanitation,

and environmental protection, can easily see the value to health-promotion schools which stress these things.

Radio and television programmes Can strongly pro-mote the ideas once good 'Health Action' pro-grammes have started in schools and can be shown to be interesting and exciting. Many programmes also exist in which children from schools promote health ideas through activities such as songs and plays. Some of these are presented by children them-selves. A book and tape, *We are on the Radio*, has been produced by the Child-to-Child Trust to help those who plan such programmes.

Musicians, film and sports personalities May be persuaded to give public support to programmes and many have done so. Be careful that those who give support set a good example themselves.

People Who Can Help at Local Level

Here the list is even longer. It includes:

Hospital doctors (usually paediatricians) These are often prepared to help on training courses. Because they have to communicate with families they are often very good with teachers.

Retired education and health workers These may often agree to serve on school health committees or to become patrons of children's health clubs.

Local business people They can help with donations of material and sometimes money for school activities. Be sure to give them the publicity they deserve for the help they have given.

Religious leaders They will be particularly interested in the way health promotion encourages children to help others, and in the new definitions of health as good social behaviour as well as good physical health.

Youth workers They will be very eager to co-operate in out-of-school activities, particularly with those which involve children who are not in school alongside schoolchildren.

Women's groups   They will welcome the way the programmes stress that boys and girls have equal responsibilities for health. The content of the health messages which stress the importance of child development and nutrition for women and girls will also help them.

Material Resources for Schools

Resources from shops and businesses   Sometimes businesses may donate goods such as seeds, soap, paper or building materials. More often they can be approached to give things which they cannot use themselves: e.g. off-cuts of wood, wire, cloth or paper for puppets or toy making, cardboard for posters and games, old newspapers and magazines for pictures to cut out.

Resources from the environment   These include grass, branches and fibre to make refuse bins and brooms; clay for models and puppets; seeds and cuttings for gardens ... and much more.

Resources from the children   Remember that children themselves are excellent resources for health, especially for learning about growth and development. Why show something on a poster if you can show it on a child!

Feel your rib cage here. Your lungs are inside it.

Written Resources

The following books are useful, relatively easy to obtain and not too expensive. If possible, programmes should buy them and make them available to programme planners and to schools.

Children for Health Available from UNICEF New York or TALC (see below.) We recommend that *Children for Health* be used alongside this book [i.e. Hawes 1997]. It is in two parts. The first part (35 pages) shows all the ways in which children become partners in health promotion in schools and from schools. The second part (135 pages) includes all the prime messages and supporting information contained in Appendix 1 of this book, which lists only the prime messages. All facts are those which are currently agreed by the World Health Organization. Each of the twelve main sections is followed by a set of objectives for children's understanding and action, activities themselves are subdivided into activities which promote *understanding* and activities which promote *action*.

Eight other important resource books

1. *Resource Book Part Two*, Child-to-Child Trust, London, 1994. Contains activity sheets under eight sub-headings, including Disability, Child Growth and Development, and Children in Especially Difficult Circumstances, which deal with topics not available or not fully treated in *Children for Health*. Each activity sheet has both factual information and suggestions for methods.

2. Feuerstein, M. T., *Partners in Evaluation*, Macmillan, London, 1986. A simple guide to those evaluating programmes.

3. Gibbs, W. and Mutunga, P., *Health into Mathematics*, Longman, Harlow, 1991. Contains many useful examples on health activities in mathematics classes for primary schools.

4. Savage, F., King, F. and Burgess, A., *Nutrition in Developing Countries*, ELBS with Oxford University Press, Oxford, 1992. Excellent, up-to-date information about all aspects of nutrition.

5. Werner, D., *Where There is No Doctor*, Macmillan, London, 1992. Comprehensive yet readable medical information.

6. Werner, D., *Disabled Village Children*, Hesperian Foundation, Palo Alto, 1987.

7. Werner, D. and Bower, B., *Helping Health Workers Learn*, Hesperian Foundation, Palo Alto, 1982. Contains a wealth of material on methodology and the organization of in-service programmes. Very easy to read.

8. Young, B. and Durston, S., *Primary Health Education*, Longman, Harlow, 1987. An excellent introduction to the teaching of health education in primary schools.

Health story books for children   A number of story books on health topics have been published by the Child-to-Child Trust and have been translated and adapted in many languages. English stories include *Child-to-Child Readers* (currently 15), published by Longman and available in bookshops or through TALC (see below).

Visual aids   TALC also publish excellent slide-sets, especially useful for teaching about health-scale, as well as a new Child-to-Child height-scale mentioned in Chapter 6.

Where to get publications   All books in English listed here are available from: Teaching-aids At Low Cost (TALC), PO Box 49, St Albans, Herts, AL1 4AX, United Kingdom. Other useful addresses for other languages include:

Arab Resource Collective (ARC), PO Box 730, Nicosia, Cyprus. (A large selection of relevant books in Arabic, including translations of many of the above.)

L'Enfant pour L'Enfant, Institut Santé et Développement, 15 rue de l'Ecole de médecine, 75572 Paris, France. (All-French material related to Child-to-Child approaches, including an excellent series of storybooks with detailed back-up notes.)

Voluntary Health Association of India (VHAI), Tong Swasthya Bhavan, 40 Institutional Area, South of IIT, New Delhi, 110 016, India. (Resources material including manuals, story books and games in English, Hindi and Indian regional languages.)

Centre for Health Education and Nutrition Awareness (CHETNA), Lilavatiben Lalbhai's Bungalow, Civil Camp Road, Shahibang,

Ahmadabad, 380 004 Gujarat, India. (Much resource material; also publishes *Children for Health* in Hindi and Gujarati. UNICEF regional and country offices.)

The Middle East Regional Office (Jordan) and the Latin American Regional Office (Columbia) have produced Arabic and Spanish versions of *Children for Health*. The office in Iran has produced a version in Farsi. These versions are available from the Facts for Life Unit, UNICEF, 3, UN Plaza, New York 10017, USA.

WHO offices and publications The Health Education and Health Promotion Unit, World Health Organization, CH-1211, Geneva 27, Switzerland (Fax 0041220 7910746) is committed to the concept of comprehensive school health promotion and publishes much relevant material, e.g. the report *Promoting Health Through Schools* WHO/HPR/HEP/96.4, December 1996.

Regional offices, especially those in India (New Delhi) and the eastern Mediterranean (Alexandria), produce locally relevant publications.

Note

1. This appendix is reprinted from Hawes 1997.

Appendix 2: Example of Child-to-Child Activity Sheets

Child-to-Child

Child-to-Child Activity Sheets are a resource for teachers, and health and community workers. They are designed to help children understand how to improve health in other children, their families and their communities. Topics chosen are important for community health and suit the age, interests and experience of children. The text, ideas and activities may be freely adapted to suit local conditions.

IMMUNISATION

THE IDEA

Every year, five million children die, and five million are disabled, from diseases which could have been prevented by immunisation against the germs which cause them. Children can understand which diseases can be prevented by immunisation, how immunisation works, and the correct immunisation schedule for themselves, their families and their friends.

People say, "Our children are not sick, so why should we take them to the clinic?"

The answer is, "Because we want to have them immunised to protect them against the most dangerous diseases of childhood."

Immunisation means making the body strong and well-prepared to fight particular diseases.

Each year, in every village and community, some babies and young children die from diseases like measles and tetanus. Others are disabled for life by diseases like polio. **This can be avoided by immunisation.**

We can look at the diseases which can be prevented by immunisation, and then we can look at how immunisation works.

Diseases that can be prevented by immunisation

Measles *Pradeep has had a high fever for six days, with red eyes, a runny nose, noisy breathing and a cough, and a rash all over. He has measles and is very ill. If he gets better, he will be weak for a long time and may catch other diseases. One of his friends became blind after being ill with measles.*

Diphtheria *Rosa breathed in some diphtheria germs which settled in her throat and made it sore. Her neck swelled. Her breathing became noisy and difficult. Then her breathing stopped and she died.*

Tuberculosis (TB) *Musa's uncle had a cough for a long time and there was blood in his spit. He coughed up the TB germs which Musa and his baby sister breathed in. The germs settled in Musa's lungs. He began to cough, lost weight, and became weak. His baby sister died.*

Tetanus *Joseph cut his foot in his field. Tetanus germs got into the wound on his foot, along with the dirt. A week later all his muscles became tight and made his body stiff. They took him to hospital, but we do not know if they can save him.*

When Vimia had her baby, they cut the cord with a dirty knife, and germs got into the cord stump. A week later the baby became stiff and stopped sucking. He later had convulsions and died.

ALL THESE DISEASES COULD HAVE BEEN PREVENTED BY IMMUNISATION.

Polio *Odongo, Opio and Akello caught polio when there was an epidemic some years ago. They and a lot of other children were ill with it. They were left paralysed and will always be disabled.*

THIS COULD HAVE BEEN PREVENTED BY IMMUNISATION

Whooping Cough *Four-year-old Amin caught whooping cough from his friends and gave it to his sister Fatima and baby Myriam. They have all been coughing, vomiting, losing weight and becoming weak. The baby goes blue with the cough and may die.*

THIS COULD HAVE BEEN PREVENTED BY IMMUNISATION

In some countries, immunisation is given against other diseases too, such as mumps and rubella, hepatitis and yellow fever. Find out from a health worker which immunisations are recommended in your country. Teach about these as well.

Immunisation is a way of stimulating the body to make enough of the right 'soldiers' (antibodies) in advance of the disease. When the germs attack, the body is ready to fight them.

How does immunisation work?

Immunisation builds protection in the body against the germs which cause these diseases. How does it do this?

When we are ill, it is because a tiny germ that can only be seen under a microscope has entered the body. The body protects and defends itself by making special 'soldiers'. These 'soldiers', which are specially armed to fight a certain germ, are called antibodies.

Sometimes, when a germ enters the body:

* the body **has not made enough** 'soldiers' or antibodies in advance, or
* the antibodies **are made too late** to prevent or fight the germ and the person will develop the disease.

If the disease is very serious, or if the child is very weak - perhaps he has been ill before, or is malnourished - there is a risk that he will die before the body can make enough antibodies to fight the disease.

A child is immunised by vaccines which are injected or given by mouth. The vaccines work by building up the child's defences . If the disease strikes before a child is immunised, immunisation is too late. All immunizations should be completed in the first year of a child's life. Half of all deaths from whooping cough, one third of all cases of polio, and a quarter of all deaths from measles, occur before the age of one year.

It is vital for infants to complete the full course of inmmunisations, otherwise the vaccines may not work. If a child is not feeling well, it is still safe to immunise them. For some diseases like polio and tetanus, the antibodies made in the body by the immunisation will not last for an entire lifetime, and so we need a second immunisation five or ten years after the first, to remind our body to make more antibodies.

When a child is immunised, the immunisation will sometimes make a small swelling, or make the child feel unwell. This is the body's way of learning to fight the disease, and nothing to worry about.

The immunisation schedule
Your country has an immunisation schedule against these diseases. Make sure that all families with children know it. Your country has decided the ages immunisation should be given (the immunisation schedule). Immunisations should be given by qualified health workers.

What is the right time for immunisation?
Schedules change with new and local knowledge. Know your own country's schedule. The following schedule is recommended by the World Health Organization (1994).

Immunisation schedule for infants*	
AGE	DISEASE TO BE IMMUNISED AGAINST
Birth	Tuberculosis (and polio in some countries)
6 weeks	Diphtheria, whooping cough, tetanus, polio
10 weeks	Diphtheria, whooping cough, tetanus, polio
14 weeks	Diphtheria, whooping cough, tetanus, polio
9 months	Measles (12-15 months in industrialized countries) and polio in some countries
	* National immunisation schedules may differ slightly from country to country

If for any reason a child has not been fully immunized in the first year of life, it is vital to have the child immunized as soon as possible.

Remember: Immunisation still helps to prevent disease even if the times between the immunisations are longer than recommended. Also remember that although it is important to be fully immunised, even some immunisation is better than none.

In many parts of the world, tetanus is the major killer of the newborn. If the mother is not immunized against tetanus, then the chance of her baby dying from the disease is one in a 100. Every woman between the ages of 15 and 44 should be fully immunized against tetanus.

IN ORDER TO STAY HEALTHY, WE MUST ALL BE IMMUNISED

ACTIVITIES

Children can find out about the immunisation activities in their community. Where is immunisation given? Are there certain days and hours for immunisation? What sort of injections are being given? (Teachers, youth workers and health workers can help children to find out this important information.)

Children can find out who needs to be immunised. Children can find out what diseases members of their family have had, and discuss them in class. Which illnesses have they had? How did it make them feel? In school, identify any children in the class and in the children's families who have not been immunised. Get children to check with their mothers and report

back. If growth charts or other records are used, sho the children where immunisation comes on the grow chart. Remind them of the dates for immunisatio Children must help their families keep immunisatic cards safe, so that they always have them when the go to the health centre.

If any young child in the class or group, or any child their families, has not been immunised, check wi health workers to see how it can be done.

Children can keep records. Children and the teachers can support the clinic by keeping records f all the families of the children in the class, or even possible for all the families in the village.

Children can help in the family. Older children ca make a birthday card to take home for a new baby the family or neighbourhood. They can hang it on t wall as a reminder. The class can help to design the card, so that it shows the right times for the local immunisation programme.

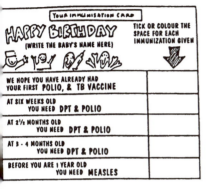

Your immunisation card		
HAPPY BIRTHDAY (WRITE THE BABY'S NAME HERE)	TICK OR COLOUR THE SPACE FOR EACH IMMUNIZATION GIVEN	
WE HOPE YOU HAVE ALREADY HAD YOUR FIRST **POLIO, & TB VACCINE**		
AT SIX WEEKS OLD YOU NEED **DPT & POLIO**		
AT 2½ MONTHS OLD YOU NEED **DPT & POLIO**		
AT 3 - 4 MONTHS OLD YOU NEED **DPT & POLIO**		
BEFORE YOU ARE 1 YEAR OLD YOU NEED **MEASLES**		

Keep reminding the mother and father to look at the baby's clinic card and the birthday card, to remind them when immunisations are due.

When the time comes, help the family to take the baby to the clinic.

During the day after immunisation, help to look after babies and comfort them if they feel unwell and cry.

Children can help in the community.

They can pass the message. Children can make birthday cards for babies, make posters, and make up songs and dances.

Children can make up plays and puppet and mime shows, such as one about a family where the children are immunised and another where they are not. Or about what happens when someone in the family who is not immunised gets one of the diseases which can be prevented.

Another play might show the unpleasant and crafty germs who wait around for those who have not been immunised. They include Measles Germ (with red spots), Polio Germ (who limps), Whooping Cough Germ and TB Germ (who cough). Some children can take the part of the Germs; others can be the antibodies.

They can help in immunisation campaigns. Children can help others to know about immunisation activities and to prepare, with adults, for the visit of the immunisation team or health worker in the community. They can show their posters and plays, and make sure that everyone in the community knows about the immunisation activities.

Immunisation times

FOLLOW-UP

Children can discuss among themselves to make sure that they all remember about the immunisation message. Have they understood it properly? Have all the children in the class been properly immunised? What about their brothers and sisters? Their parents?

Children can count how many people disabled by polio there are in their age group; how many there are among people who are ten years older; twenty years older. Is there a difference? Why?

Children can try and ask their grandparents what happened before immunisation.

USING THIS SHEET

Teachers, including religious teachers, **youth group leaders** and **community development workers** could introduce these ideas to groups of children, if possible with help from **health workers**. It is important for children really to understand about immunisation if they are to pass on the message and help their families and communities. **It is important for teachers and youth leaders to give the message regularly and not just once.**

For further information, please contact:
Child-to-Child, Institute of Education,
University of London, 20 Bedford Way,
London WC1H 0AL, U.K.

References

Aarons, A., H. Hawes and J. Gayton (1979) *CHILD-to-child*, Basingstoke: Macmillan.

Aikman, S. (1994a) 'School curriculum as a forum for articulating intercultural relations with particular reference to the Peruvian Amazon', in E. Thomas (ed.) (1994), *International Perspectives on Schooling: A Symposium Proceedings*, Institute of Education, University of London.

— (1994b) 'Intercultural education and Harakmbut identity: a case study of the community of San José in Southeastern Peru', PhD thesis, Institute of Education, University of London.

Anderson, C. A. and M. J. Bowman (eds) (1966) *Education and Economic Development*, London: Frank Cass.

Anderson, R. (1984) 'Health Promotion: an Overview', *European Monographs in Health Education Research*, 6 (4): 4–126, Scottish Health Education Group, Edinburgh.

Apple, M. W. (ed.) (1982) *Cultural and Economic Reproduction in Education*, London: Routledge and Kegan Paul.

Arnstein, S. R. (1971) 'Eight rungs on the ladder of citizen participation', in E. Cahn and M. Possett, *Citizen Participation: Effecting Community Change*, New York: Praeger.

Babugura, A. K., R. Monau and J. Butale (1993) 'The CHILD-to-child Programme of Botswana: an Evaluation', *Report for UNICEF (Gaborone)*, Gaborone: UNICEF.

Baric, L. (1985) 'The meaning of words: health promotion', *Journal of the Institute of Health Education*, 23: 10–15.

— (1995) *Health Promotion and Education Module 1: Problems and Solutions*, 3rd edn, Altrincham: Barns Publications.

Barnard, A. (1993) *Hunters and Herders of Southern Africa*, Cambridge: Cambridge University Press.

Beattie, A., M. Gott, L. Jones and M. Sidell (eds) (1993) *Health and Wellbeing: A Reader*, London: Macmillan.

Bernstein, H. (1979) 'Sociology of underdevelopment vs Sociology of development?' in D. Lehmann (ed.), *Development Theory*, London: Frank Cass.

Bhalerao, V. R. (1981) 'School children as health leaders in the family', *World Health Forum*, 2 (2): 209–10.

Blaug, M. (1985). 'Where are we now in the economics of education?' *Economics of Education Review*, 4 (1): 17–28.

Bomba, W., M. Chaika, F. Chisala, V. Ekatan et al. (1994) 'Report of the Workshop on Health through the School', Swaziland, 21–25 March 1994, unpublished report, Manchester: British Council.

Borini, G. (1986). 'Health and development: a marriage of heaven and hell?', *Studies in Third World Societies* 34, Williamsburg, VA: College of William and Mary, Department of Anthropology.

Bowles, S. and H. Gintis (1976) *Schooling in Capitalist America: Educational Reform and the Contradictions of Economic Life*, New York: Basic Books.

Bruner, J. S. (1961) 'The act of discovery', *Harvard Educational Review*, 1 (1).

— 1974) *Beyond the Information Given. Studies in the Psychology of Knowing*, London: Allen and Unwin.

— (1977) *The Process of Education*, Cambridge, MA: Harvard University Press.

Bundy, D. and A. Hall (1992) *International Partnership for School Child Development*, summary report of the Next Steps meeting, UNDP, New York, 7–8 January, Scientific Coordinating Centre for the International Partnership, University of London, Imperial College.

Caldwell, J. (1986) 'Routes to low mortality in poor countries', *Population and Development Review*, 12 (2).

— (1993) 'Health transition: the cultural, social and behavioural determinants of health in the Third World', *Social Science and Medicine*, 36 (2): 125–36

Campbell, Main & Associates (1991) 'Western Sandveld remote area dwellers', unpublished report for the Botswana Ministry of Local Government and Lands and the Norwegian Agency for International Development.

Carlisle, J. (1988) *Toys for Fun*, London: Macmillan.

Carnegie, R. (1991) 'Child-to-Child: an analysis of an innovative approach to health education in developing countries', unpublished MSc thesis, University of Sussex.

Carnegie, R. and H. Hawes (eds) (1990) *Child-to-Child and the Growth and Development of Young Children*, London: Child-to-Child.

Carnoy, M. (1974) *Education and Cultural Imperialism*, London: Longman.

Carr-Hill, R. (1994a) 'Cultural conditionality on aid to basic education', in E. Thomas (ed.), *International Perspectives on Culture and Schooling*, Department of International and Comparative Education, Institute of Education, University of London.

— 1994b) 'An assessment of the demographic impact of AIDS on the education system', in P. Pridmore and E. Chase, *Aids as an Educational Issue*, DICE Occasional Papers No. 12: 7–10, Institute of Education, University of London.

Chambers, R. (1983). *Rural Development: Putting the Last First*, London: Longman.

CHETNA (1990) *Learning for Life*, report of a workshop organized by CHET-NA in New Delhi, 24–26 April 1990, Ahmedabad: CHETNA.

CHILD-to-child (1978) *Report of the Meeting held at Fittleworth*, London: Child-to-Child.

Child-to-Child (1990) *Twelve Years on: A Child-to-Child Consultative Meeting*, London: Child-to-Child.

— (1992) *Education for Health in Schools and Teachers' Colleges*, London: Child-to-Child.

— (1993a) *A Directory of Child-to-Child Activities in Kenya*, London: Child-to-Child.

— (1993b) *A Directory of Child-to-Child Activities Worldwide*, London: Child-to-Child.

— (1993c) *A Directory of Child-to-Child Activities in Tanzania*, London: Child-to-Child.

— (1994) *A Directory of Child-to-Child Activities in Tanzania*, London: Child-to-Child.

— (1996) *A Directory of Child-to-Child Activities Worldwide*, London: Child-to-Child.

— (1994a) *Resource Book Part One*, London: Child-to-Child.

— (1994b) *Resource Book Part Two*, London: Child-to-Child.

— (1995) 'Child-to-Child in the southern states of India 28 February to 2 March 1995', unpublished report of a networking meeting, London: Child-to-Child.

— (1996) *Report of a Consultative Meeting*, London: Child-to-Child.

Child-to-Child/ICCB (1997) *Listening for Health*, London: Child-to-Child.

Chiwela, J. M. (1996) 'The Child-to-Child programme: development and mapping assessment report of the developmental level of Child-to-Child programme in Zambia', unpublished report, London: Child-to-Child.

Clay, M. M. and B. Watson (1982) 'An inservice program for reading recovery teachers', in *Observing Young Readers*, selected papers, London: Heinemann Educational.

Cochran, A. L. (1971) *Effectiveness and Efficiency*, London: Nuffield Provincial Hospitals Trust.

Cochrane, S. H. (1979) *Fertility and Education: What Do We Really Know?*,

World Bank Staff Working Paper no. 26, Baltimore, MD: Johns Hopkins University Press.

Cochrane, S., J. Leslie and D. O'Hara (1982) *The Effects of Education on Health*, World Bank Staff Working Paper no. 405, Washington, DC: World Bank.

Colclough, C., P. Rose and M. Tembon (1998) 'Gender inequalities in primary schooling: the roles of poverty and adverse cultural practice', unpublished paper presented at Gender and Education Seminar, University of Reading, August 1998.

Coombs, P. H. (1968) *The World Crisis in Education: A Systems Analysis*, London: Oxford University Press.

Cornia, G. A., R. Jolly and F. Stewart (1987) *Adjustment with a Human Face: Protecting the Vulnerable and Promoting Growth*, Oxford: Oxford University Press

Croall, J. (1983) *Neill of Summerhill*, London: Routledge and Kegan Paul.

Dewey, J. (1964) *Democracy and Education*, New York: Macmillan.

DFID (1997) *Eliminating World Poverty: A Challenge to the 21st Century, White Paper on International Development*, London: HMSO.

Dhillon, H. S. and D. Tolsma (1992) *Meeting Global Health Challenges: A Position Paper on Health Education*, International Union for Health Education and the Division of Health Education, Geneva: WHO.

Dore, R. (1976) *The Diploma Disease*, London: George Allen and Unwin.

Downie, R. S., C. Fyfe and A. Tannahill (1990) *Health Promotion Models and Values*, Oxford: Oxford University Press.

Doyal, L. (1979) *The Political Economy of Health*, London: Pluto.

Dubos, R. (1979) *Mirage of Health*, New York: Harper Colophon.

Durkheim, E. (1977) *The Evolution of Educational Thought*, London: Routledge and Kegan Paul.

Eraut, M., L. Goad and G. Smith (1975) *The Analysis of Curriculum Material*, Occasional Paper 2, University of Sussex.

Evans, J. (1993) *Participatory Evaluation of Child-to-Child Projects in India Funded by the Aga Khan Foundation*, Geneva: Aga Khan Foundation.

Ewles, L. and I. Simnett (1985) *Promoting Health. A Practical Guide to Health Education*, Chichester: John Wiley.

Fagerlind and Saha (1989) *Education and National Development*, 2nd edn, Oxford: Pergamon.

Faure, E., F. Herrera, A. Kaddoura, H. Lopes, M. Rahnema and F. Champion Ward (1972) *Learning to Be: The World of Education Today and Tomorrow*, Paris: UNESCO.

Feuerstein, M. T. (1981) *Report of the Evaluation of the Child-to-Child Programme, March–September 1981*, London: Child to Child.

Foot, H., M. Morgan and R. Shute (eds) (1990) *Children Helping Children,* Developmental Psychology and its Applications series, Chichester: John Wiley.

Francis, V. (1993) 'Health education – a key to community eye health: but where are the locksmiths?', *Community Eye Health,* 6 (12): 17–19.

Freire, P. (1972) *Pedagogy of the Oppressed,* Harmondsworth: Penguin.

— (1997) *Pedagogy of Hope,* New York: Continuum.

French, J. and L. Adams (1986) 'From analysis to synthesis: theories of health education', *Health Education Journal,* 45: 71–4.

Froebel, F. (1985, first published 1895) *Friedrich Froebel's Pedagogics of the Kindergarten: or his Ideas Concerning the Play and Playthings of the Child,* New York: D. Appleton, International Education Series.

Fryer, M. L. (1991) 'Health education through interactive radio – a Child-to-Child project in Bolivia', *Health Education Quarterly,* 18 (1): 65–77.

Gardner, G. (1995) 'Third World debt still growing', in *Vital Signs 1995: The Trends that are Shaping Our Future,* New York: Worldwatch Institute.

Gibbs, W. (1993) *Child-to-Child in Zambia: Evaluation Report,* London: Child-to-Child.

— (1997) 'Evaluation of the Child-to-Child programme in Zambia', unpublished report, Zambia: UNICEF:.

Gibbs, W. and P. Mutunga (1991) *Health into Mathematics,* Harlow: Longman.

Green, L. and J. Raeburn (1988) 'Health promotion. What is it? What will it become?', *Health Promotion,* 3 (2): 151–9.

Green, L. W. and M. W. Kreuter (1991) *Health Education Planning: An Educational and Environmental Approach,* 2nd edn, California: Mayfield.

Guthrie, D. (1991) Interview data.

Hallak, J. (1990) *Investing in the Future Setting Educational Priorities in the Developing World,* Oxford: Pergamon.

Hanbury, C. (ed.) (1993) *Child-to Child and Children Living in Camps,* London: Child-to-Child.

Hanbury, C. and S. McCrum (undated) *We are on the Radio,* London: Child-to-Child.

— (1995) *Child-to-Child Training Pack,* London: Child-to-Child.

Harber, C. and L. Davies (1997) *School Management and Effectiveness in Developing Countries: The Post-Bureaucratic School,* London: Cassell.

Hart, R. (1992) 'Children's participation: from tokenism to citizenship', *Innocenti Essay,* no. 4, New York: UNICEF.

— (1997) *Children's Participation: The Theory and Practice of Involving Young Children in Community Development and Environmental Care,* London: Earthscan.

Hawes, C. (1993) *How to Use the Child-to-Child Readers: A Guide for Teachers*, London: Longman.

Hawes, H. (1979) *Curriculum and Reality of African Primary Schools*, Harlow: Longman.

— (1988) *Child-to-Child: Another Path to Learning*, Hamburg: UNESCO Institute of Education.

— (1991) Interview data.

— (1992) 'Reflections on the interpretation and implementation of the Child-to-Child approach', unpublished paper, London: Child-to-Child.

— (1993) 'Report on workshop on health into language', unpublished report, London: Child-to-Child.

— (1997) *Health Promotion in Our Schools*, London: Child-to-Child.

Hawes, H. and D. Morley (1988) 'Child-to-Child: a worldwide network in health education', unpublished conference paper, 17 March, London: Child-to-Child.

Hawes, H. and C. Scotchmer (1993) *Children for Health*, London: Child-to-Child.

Hawes, H. and D. Stephens (1990) *Questions of Quality: Primary Education and Development*, London: Longman.

Heslop, M. (1991) *Child-to-Child Review of Literature and Research*, London: Child-to-Child.

Hobcraft, J. N. (1993) 'Women's education, child welfare and child survival: a review of the evidence', *Health Transition Review*, 13(2).

Hunter, J. M., L. Rey, K. Y. Chu, E. O. Ade Kolu-John and K. E. Mott (1993) *Parasitic Diseases in Water Resources Development: the Need for Intersectoral Negotiation*, Geneva: WHO.

IIED (1995) *Notes on Participatory Learning and Action*, PLA Notes, no. 23, London: International Institute for Environment and Development.

— (1996) PLA *Notes*, no. 25, special issue on children's participation, pp. 30–87, London: International Institute for Environment and Development.

Illich, I. (1973) *Deschooling Society*, Harmondsworth: Penguin.

— (1976) 'The epidemics of modern medicine' in I. Illich, *Limits to Medicine*, London: Marion Boyars.

Inkeles, A. and D. Smith (1974) *Becoming Modern*, London: Heinemann.

Institute of Christian Leadership (1987) *Child-to-Child in Zambia*, Mipika, Zambia: Institute for Christian Leadership.

Ivanovic, D. (1991) 'Nutrition and education III: educational achievement and nutrient intake of Chilean elementary and high school graduates', *Archivos Latinameri de nutricion*, 41: 499–515.

Joseph, M. V. (1980) 'Teachers and pupils as health workers', *The Lancet*, November, 8: 1016.

Kann, U. (1989) *Achieving Universal Basic Education in Botswana – the Barriers, and Some Suggestions for Overcoming Them*, Gaborone: National Institute of Development Research and Documentation, University of Botswana.

Kickbush, I. (1986) 'Health promotion: a global perspective', *Canadian Journal of Public Health*, 77: 321–6.

— (1990) *A Strategy for Health Promotion*, Copenhagen: WHO Regional Office for Europe.

Knight, J., S. Grantham-McGregor and S. Ismail (1991) 'A Child-to-Child programme in rural Jamaica', *Child: Care, Health and Development*, 17 (1): 49–58.

Komba, D., A. Ayoub and R. M. Issa (1997) 'Impact evaluation of the Child-to-Child health education project in Zanzibar', unpublished document, Zanzibar: Aga Khan Foundation.

LaFond, A. (1995) *Sustaining Primary Health Care*, London: Earthscan.

Lansdown, R. (1995) *Child-to-Child: A Review of the Literature*, London: Child-to-Child.

Leach, F. (1994) 'Expatriates as agents of cross-cultural transmission', in E. Thomas (ed.), *International Perspectives on Culture and Schooling*, Department of International and Comparative Education, Institute of Education, University of London.

Lee, R. B. (1984) *The Dobe !Kung*. Case Studies in Cultural Anthropology, Orlando: Harcourt, Brace, Jovanovich.

Levinger, B. (1994) *Nutrition, Health and Education for All*, New York: Education and Development Centre and UNDP.

Lewin, K. (1993) *Education and Development: The Issues and the Evidence*, ODA Education Research Occasional Paper Series, Serial no. 6.

Lewin, K., A. Little and C. Colclough (1983a) 'Effects of education on development objectives', *Prospects*, XIII (3).

— (1983b) 'Effects of education on development objectives (II)', *Prospects*, XIII (4).

Little, A. (1992) *Education and Development: Macro Relationships and Micro Cultures*, Silver Jubilee Paper 4, Institute of Development Studies, Sussex.

Little A. and R. Dore (1982) *The Diploma Disease* (a resource book for the film), *Institute of Development Studies Discussion Paper 180*, Sussex: IDS.

Little, A. and C. Yates (eds) (1991) 'Education and development', External Diploma in Distance Education, Course 1, Block A, Unit 1, Unpublished Document, London: University of London Institute of Education/International Extension College, Cambridge.

Liverpool Public Health Annual Report (1995), Liverpool: Liverpool Health Authority.

Lockheed, M. E. and A. Verspoor, (1991) *Improving Primary Education in Developing Countries*, Washington, DC: World Bank.

References 183

Luswata, S. M. (1992) *Child-to-Child Uganda Evaluation Report*, Kampala: UNICEF.

McClelland, D. (1961) *The Achieving Society*, London: D. Van Nostrand.

Macdonald, J. (1993) *Primary Health Care: Medicine in its Place*, London: Earthscan.

McKeown, T. (1976) *The Modern Rise of Population*, London: Edward Arnold.

— (1979) *The Role of Medicine: Dream, Mirage or Nemesis?*, Oxford: Blackwell.

Marshall, L. (1976) *The !Kung of Nyae Nyae*, London: Harvard University Press.

Martorell, R. (1992) 'Long-term effects of improved childhood nutrition', *SCN NEWS*, 8: 10–12, New York: UN ACC/SCN.

Masolotate, L. (1997) *CHILD-to-child Network of Botswana: a History and Analysis*, Gaborone: Child-to-Child Network of Botswana.

Measham, A. (1986) 'Health and development: the Bank's experience', *Finance and Development*, December, New York: IMF and World Bank.

Mogalakwe, M. (1986) *Inside Ghanzi Freehold Farms. A Look at the Conditions of Farm Workers*, Gaborone, Botswana: Botswana Government Ministry of Local Government and Lands, Applied Research Unit.

Mogwe, A. (1992) *Who Was (T)here First? An Assessment of the Human Rights Situation of Basarwa in Selected Communities in the Gantsi District, Botswana'*, Occasional Paper no. 10, Gaborone: Botswana Christian Council.

Montessori, M. (1918a) *The Advanced Montessori Method. Part 1: Theory of Spontaneous Activity*, London: Heinemann.

— (1918b) *The Advanced Montessori Method. Part 2. The Montessori Elementary Material*, London: Heinemann.

Montgomery, S. M. and I. Schoon (1997) 'Health and health behaviour', in J. Bynner, E. Ferri and P. Shepherd (eds) *Twentysomething in the 1990s: Getting On, Getting By, Getting Nowhere*, Aldershot: Ashgate.

Morley, D. (1993) personal communication.

Morley, D. and H. Lovel (1986) *My Name is Today*, London: Macmillan.

Morley, D. and P. Pridmore (1993) 'Health education: where does the doctor come in?' *Africa Health*, September, Cambridge: FSG Communications.

Mortimore, P. and G. Whitty (1997) *Can School Improvement Overcome the Effects of Disadvantage?*, London: Institute of Education, University of London.

Mullen, P. D. and P. Zapaka (1989) 'Assessing the quality of health promotion programs', *HMO Practice*, 3: 98–103.

Navarro, V. (1984) 'The underdevelopment of health or the health of underdevelopment: an analysis of the distribution of human health resources in Latin America', *International Journal of Health Services*, 4: 5.

Odaga, A. and W. Heneveld (1995) *Girls and Schools in Sub-Saharan Africa: From Analysis to Action*, Washington, DC: World Bank.

Oxenham, J. (1991) 'Education, learning, literacy and schooling', External Diploma in Distance Education, Course 1, Block A, Unit 1, unpublished document, International Extension College/University of London Institute of Education, Department of International and Comparative Education, London.

Phillips, D. R. and Y. Verhasselt (1994) *Health and Development*, London: Routledge.

Phinney, R. and J. Evans (1992/3) 'From child to child: children as communicators', in *Development Communication Report*, 78: 7–9, Arlington, VA: Clearinghouse on Development Communication.

Piaget, J. (1970) 'Piaget's theory', in P. Mussen (ed.), *Carmichael's Manual of Child Psychology*, vol. 1, New York: Wiley.

Pollitt, E. (1984) *Nutrition and Educational Achievement*, Nutrition Education Series, 9, Paris: UNESCO.

— (1990) *Malnutrition and Infection in the Classroom*, Paris: UNESCO.

Portes, A. (1973) 'Modernity and development: a critique', *Studies in Comparative International Development*, VIII (3): 247–79.

Pridmore, P. (1996) 'Children as health educators: the Child-to-Child approach', unpublished PhD thesis. University of London, Institute of Education.

— (1999) *Participatory Approaches to Health Promotion in Schools: A Child-to-Child Training Manual*, London: Child-to-Child.

Pridmore, P. and B. Smith (1996) 'Health through the school', unpublished report for the British Council on a workshop conducted for the East African Region, Nairobi: British Council.

Psacharopoulos, G. (1985) 'Returns to education: a further international update and implications', *Journal of Human Resources*, XX: 583–604.

Putnam, R. D., R. Leonardi and R. Y. Nanetti (1993) *Making Democracy Work: Civic Traditions in Modern Italy*, Princeton, NJ: Princeton University Press.

Rawson, D. (1992) 'The growth of health promotion theory and its rational reconstruction: lessons from the philosophy of science', in R. Bunton and G. Macdonald, *Health Promotion: Disciplines and Diversity*, London: Routledge.

Republic of Uganda/UNICEF (1994) *Situational Analysis of the Situation of Women and Children*, Kampala: UNICEF.

Rhode, J. E. and T. Sadjinum (1980) 'Elementary school children as health educators: role of school health programmes in primary health care', *The Lancet*, 1: 1350–2.

Rogers, A. (1996) *Teaching Adults*, Buckingham: Open University Press.

Rousseau, J. J. (1762) *Emile* (1966 English trans.), London: Everyman's Library.

Sanders, D. (1985) *The Struggle for Health*, London: Macmillan.

Saugestad, S. (1993) 'Botswana: the inconvenient indigenous peoples', *IWGIA Newsletter,* 2, available from International Work Group for Indigenous Affairs, Fiolstraede 10, DK-11711, Copenhagen K, Denmark.

Schultz, T. W. (1961) 'Investment in human capital', *American Economic Review,* 51, March: 1–17.

— (1971) *Investment in Human Capital,* New York: The Free Press.

Seers, D. (1969) 'The meaning of development', unpublished paper presented to the Eleventh World Conference of the Society for International Development, New Delhi.

Shaeffer, S. (1994) 'The impact of HIV on education systems', in P. Pridmore and E. Chase, *Aids as an Educational Issue,* DICE Occasional Papers no. 12, University of London, Institute of Education.

Sharma, S. and A. Wadhwa (1988) *Child-to-Child Programme Evaluation: Delhi Project,* New Delhi: Lady Irwin College.

Silberbauer, G. B. (1981) *Hunter and Habitat in the Central Kalahari Desert,* Cambridge: Cambridge University Press.

Somerset, H. C. A. (1987) *Child-to-Child: A Survey,* London: Child-to-Child.

Stephens, D. (1998) *Girls and Basic Education: A Cultural Enquiry,* Education Research Papers, London: Department for International Development (DFID).

— (1993) 'Putting children first – an alternative approach to health education in India and Uganda: research in progress', unpublished paper presented at the BATROE Conference on the Changing Role of the State in Educational Development, Oxford: 24–28 September 1993.

— (1996) 'Child-to-Child: an investigation into the experiences of children and teachers in Uganda', research monograph, London: Child-to-Child Trust.

— (1997) 'Quality of primary education', in K. Watson et al. (eds), *Education Dilemmas: Debate and Diversity,* Vol. 4, *Quality in Education,* London: Cassell.

Stewart, F. (1991) 'Education and adjustment: the experience of the 1980s and lessons for the 1990s', mimeo, London: Commonwealth Secretariat.

Sutherland, M. (1988) *Theory of Education,* Harlow: Longman.

Tones K., S. Tilford and Y. Robinson (1990) *Health Education: Effectiveness and Efficiency,* London: Chapman and Hall.

UN ACC/SCN (1990) 'Some options for improving nutrition in the 1990s', supplement to *SCN News,* no. 7, February.

UNCRC (1989) *Convention on the Rights of the Child,* New York: UN.

UNDP (1990) *Human Development Report 1990,* New York: Oxford University Press.

UNICEF (1989) *Facts for Life,* New York: UNICEF.

— (1991) *The State of the World's Children,* New York: UNICEF.

— (1992) *The State of the World's Children*, New York: UNICEF.

— (1996) *Childscope Monitoring and Process Report*, Accra: UNICEF.

— (1997) *The State of the World's Children*, New York: UNICEF.

Van der Vynckt, S. (1992/3) 'Primary school health: where are we and where are we going?', *International Journal of Health Education*, *Hygie*, X: 48–50.

Vulliamy, G., K. Lewin and D. Stephens (1990) *Doing Educational Research in Developing Countries*, Basingstoke: Falmer.

Ward, F. C. (ed.) (1974) *Education and Development Reconsidered*, London: Praeger.

WCEFA (World Conference on Education for All) (1990) *World Declaration on Education for All and Framework for Action to Meet Basic Learning Needs*, New York: Inter-agency Commission.

Weil, C., A. P. Busan, J. F. Wilson, M. R. Reich and D. J. Bradley (1990) *The Impact of Development Policies on Health. A Review of the Literature*, Geneva: WHO.

Werner, D. (1977). 'The village health worker – lackey or liberator?', paper prepared for the International Hospital Federation Congress Sessions on Health Auxiliaries and the Health Team, Tokyo, 22–27 May, reprinted in N. Black, D. Boswell, A. Gray, S. Murphy and J. Popay (1984) *Health and Disease*, Milton Keynes: Open University Press, p. 182.

Werner, D. and B. Saunders (1997) *Questioning the Solution: The Politics of Primary Health Care and Child Survival*, Palo Alto, CA: Health Rights – Workgroup for People's Health and Rights.

Whitehead, A. N. (1932) *The Aims of Education and Other Essays*, London: Williams and Norgate.

WHO (1978) *Alma-Ata 1978 Primary Health Care*, Health for All series no. 1, Geneva: WHO.

— (1984) *Report of the Working Group on Concepts and Principles of Health Promotion*, Copenhagen: WHO.

— (1986) *Ottawa Charter for Health Promotion*, Copenhagen: WHO Regional Office for Europe.

— 1988) *From Alma-Ata to the Year 2000: Reflections at the Midpoint*, Geneva: WHO.

— (1992a) 'Comprehensive school health education: suggested guidelines for action', WHO/UNESCO/UNICEF unpublished document, Geneva: WHO, Division of Health Education and Promotion.

— (1992b) *Our Planet Our Earth: Report of the WHO Commission on Health and the Environment*, Geneva: WHO.

— (1993) *Report of the Meeting between the WHO and the Partnership for Child Development*, WHO document WHO/CDS/PIP/94. 1. Geneva: WHO Division of Communicable Diseases.

— (1994) 'The World Health Organization's school health initiative', unpublished document, Health Education and Promotion Unit of the Division of Health Promotion and Education, Geneva: WHO.

— (1996) 'Research to improve implementation and effectiveness of school health programmes', unpublished document, Geneva: WHO Health Education and Promotion Unit.

— (1997) *Promoting Health through Schools: Report of a WHO Expert Committee on Comprehensive School Health Education and Promotion*, WHO Technical Report Series 870, Geneva: WHO.

Wilkinson, R. G. (1996) *Unhealthy Societies: The Afflictions of Inequality*, London: Routledge.

World Bank (1992) *World Development Report*, Oxford: Oxford University Press.

— (1993) *World Development Report: Investing in Health*, Oxford: Oxford University Press.

Zaveri, S. (1988) 'Evaluation of Bombay Child-to-Child project', unpublished document, Bombay: Centre for Research and Development.

Index